ALL IN THE BABY POOL:

REMEMBERING TEMPE BEACH

SALLY COLE

To the Lifeguards
Who kept us safe

Table of Contents

Preface

In 1963 I became a freshman at Tempe High where, caught up in the thrill of being finally a real teen, I forgot about the summer past, hanging out at Tempe Beach. Had I known when summer came again the pool would be gone, I'm not sure how long I would have mourned. Meet the Beatles had just been released, and the lifeguards (our first "boy band") didn't stand a chance against the mop-tops that were George, Ringo, John, and Paul. We each chose our favorite (John) and learned the songs we would never hear on the jukebox by the snack bar at our hometown pool. Perhaps because I was partial to John, I loved his creation "In My Life," with its celebration of people and place. Some forty years later I would hear it sung by my daughter's high-school chorus in New Orleans, its opening words on the spot engendering the feeling that my son Davy calls "saudade," a Portuguese term for a longing too intense for words: "There are places I'll remember all my life/Though some have changed./Some forever not for better./Some have gone, and some remain."

For me that memorable place—hands down—is Tempe Beach, the pool whose allure I decided one day could be captured in words. I had the title from the start. What I hadn't grasped was the frailty of memory, the dissipation after fifty years of names, dates—even aspects of the pool itself: the tilt of the bathhouse, facing neither First nor Mill; the number and location of the life-guard chairs; the menu of the snack-bar stand. And so by necessity I tracked down those who had

iii

swum there too, who had worked in the bathhouse or manned that snack bar, who had guarded from those chairs, who had been on the swim team or just pedaled cross town for a day of swimming in the sun.

Their recall was flawed as well. And yet in sum—in that misremembered aggregate—I hoped to approximate the place once referred to as the "brilliant star in Tempe's crown." For those years too long ago for any to recall, I scoured through old newspapers, oral histories saved on tape, manuscripts, and history books. What emerged was a hybrid, a kind of history/collective memoir: subjective, colloquial, sometimes, maybe, wrong. And yet it seemed right to do it this way. Joe Spracale—swim coach, life-guard—said in remembering Tempe Beach, "On Sundays it was body-to-body people. You couldn't move." My book, then, I thought, would be cover-to-cover voices that would capture, like a visual poem, the essence of its subject. Tempe Beach was a communal place. Its tale would be communal too.

I hope someone follows up my effort and writes another volume on Tempe Beach: a conventional history, a memoir, a story cycle, a poem. Until then, I hope Tempeans will enjoy remembering this unique place and that others will be enlightened to the fact that it once was there—a long, blue icy pool—in that now-barren space that is Tempe Beach Park.

Introduction

Before the waters of Tempe Town Lake ran through the Salt River bed dividing Tempe, Arizona, from its sister city Scottsdale; before a modern bathhouse and puddle-like swimming pool inhabited the site between First Street and the river bottom; there lay in that same spot an Olympic-sized swimming pool with high and low diving boards and a smooth-stoned bathhouse known as Tempe Beach. All summer long the city's children swam and dived there, plunged in after popsicle sticks in the game known as Dibble Dabble, slathered themselves with iodine and baby oil and sunbathed in the grass beside the snack bar where five cents would buy a square of ice-cream taffy, and the jukebox pumped out in unbroken sequence the heartbreak of the Everly Brothers' "Cathy's Clown" and the cartoon staccato of "Alley Oop." Presiding over this children's world, a crew of bronzed lifeguards in red swim trunks—whistles around their necks, zinc oxide covering their noses—rotated from deep end to mid-pool to baby pool, reining in the hi-jinks of pre-pubescent boys and enforcing the few rules (no running, no swimming under the diving boards) while making sure those in the deep end could document their right to be there by swimming across the pool.

It was a Charlie Brown world, except for those lifeguards, an adult-free zone. The sun beat down on the city's children, the water shimmered, the jukebox played its endless tunes, punctuated by the rattle of the diving boards, the deep boom and splash of a cannonball or figure-four, the whistle of a lifeguard.

1

Those of us who spent our youth there can call up those days from decades hence, can still smell the pool-deck under our noses where we lay to warm ourselves, the hamburgers frying; can still feel the slap of a misdive from the high board and that icy plunge into first-day water (the pool was drained and refilled every few days). As the week progressed, the water grew a warmer, deeper blue as its chlorine content burned our eyes and the lane markers blurred beneath its surface. The popsicle sticks in our Dibble Dabble games rose more slowly to the surface. We grew older. And now we remember.

First-Day Water

Memoir

I can track the time-line of my days at Tempe Beach by the swimsuit I was wearing. My earliest memory is of a white one-piece with three lines of black stitching down the front. It must have been the summer of 1960. My friend Laure wore an identical suit; we had picked them out together in that preteen stage when girls proclaim their solidarity by wearing matching outfits. In fourth grade we had carried this tendency to its extreme by creating a secret society called The Pink Shadow Club. One day a week Laure and I, along with the girls we'd allowed to join, wore a uniform we'd devised ourselves: a white blouse, white shorts with a strip of pink bias tape sewed along each side seam, a pink-felt badge, and atop our heads a white sailor's cap (probably a tribute to those Shirley Temple movies we'd devour on the weekends) with the pink embroidered letters "PSC."

As I recall, we had a secret hand sign to reinforce our exclusivity. During the pledge, our right hands over our hearts, our left arms at our sides, we'd subtly lift our left hands out approximately forty-five degrees. I'm not sure anyone noticed this, but we did drive our classmates crazy by refusing to disclose the meaning of "PSC." We also tortured other girls by flaunting our membership in this club, thus confirming the age-old tendency of men (and certainly women) to bolster their own fragile claims to rank by creating an out-group, an action I remember at the time as producing a strange mix of pleasure and pain, particularly pain when we black-balled a girl named Gwen, whom we both liked.

I'm not sure why we did this, except that we had to. Not only were we carrying that hard-wired human impulse to shun—to scapegoat—but if everyone could join there would be no club. At one point someone deciphered the cryptic code of "PSC," so we changed our name to The Pink Swan Club, somehow managing to keep that one under wraps. And then the whole craze died as suddenly as it had begun, leaving just Laure and me in matching swim suits that summer at Tempe Beach.

We arrived unencumbered: a towel and a popsicle stick, the former to counteract the chill of the water, the latter to keep us entertained. In those days, all it took was that stick and a group of three or four to fill up the afternoon. One girl would put the popsicle stick between her toes and jump into the deep end, carrying the stick down ten feet to the bottom, where she would use her hand to place it there, then ascend as fast as possible to join the others on the pool's edge, watching for the first golden glint of the stick on its way to the surface. First one girl, having sighted it, then another and another would plunge in after the stick; the one to connect would signal her success by calling out, "Dibble Dabble," and so the game went on as the victor would take the stick back down to reset the game.

When the pool had just been filled, the game moved faster, the water so clear–not a hint of blue—that every speck on the bottom seemed but inches away: the lane lines sharp-edged, the popsicle stick, even ten feet down, so apparent that the girl resurfacing could barely climb out before the others would plunge in, with one victorious, shouting out "Dibble Dabble." That cry defines for me the sound of Tempe Beach as much as the jukebox and the lifeguards' whistles, the voice of a girl in her simple game.

At some point in the summer, to augment Dibble Dabble, Laure and I devised a sort of Water Badge, to be earned by accomplishing a series of tasks. I remember only two: "Do Sally's Special Across the Pool and Back," and "Jump Off the High Board Without Hesitation." Laure had been careful to append "without hesitation" to that feat, the high board likely to engender second thoughts. Sally's Special was my own creation, a kind of mid-pool locomotion involving a plunge under water, bent-kneed, and then a push up off the bottom at a forward angle to the surface where, taking a breath, I would repeat the motion. I remember using this method to cross the pool with only a modicum of effort, the push off the bottom replacing the strain of the crawl for one so thin, so lacking in buoyancy. Whether we ever completed the full array of tasks, I don't recall, nor whether we created an actual badge, like those pink felt ones of the PSC, to mark the event. But that memory defines for me the simplicity of those days, the ability to entertain ourselves with no adult supervision, our creativity on those long summer afternoons.

I remember sometimes, in the evening, being driven across the Mill Avenue Bridge and seeing from my passenger's seat the newly drained pool below, at the bottom of which a line of lifeguards—some three abreast with push brooms—would be mucking out the pool. I knew then the next day the water would be clean and cold, the cycle renewed, for the week then had

7

seasons, the wintery blue of fifth-day water giving way to a kind of Spring.

By mid-summer my skin had turned a deep red-brown, set off by that white suit, so that sometimes people would address me in Spanish. Laure's hair had turned a faint chlorine-green, as had that of all the blondes. I don't recall a single fight or even disagreement that summer, just an endless cycle of harmony. We plunged and resurfaced. The lifeguards made their slow circle from chair to chair around the pool. The jukebox played. The sun was hot, the water cold, so cold— especially when the pool had just been filled with first-day water.

History

1923-1933
The First Decade of Tempe Beach

Tempe Historical Museum
Reflections on Tempe Beach
Exhibition Photo/Exhibition Graph
Reproduction Number: 34
Harold Vogel Collection
Date: circa 1932

Although first-day water would always be at least a weekly feature of Tempe Beach, only one day's water could claim that title in a literal sense, that of July 11th, 1923, the day the pool opened for the very first time. I remember my father telling us his greatest disappointment in life, that he was born too late to go with Lewis and Clark on their journey through that pristine land. I envision this huge pool the very same way then, as unspoilt territory yet to be explored. If I were to envy anyone who swam that day it would be William Windes, the boy who, unable to wait for the pool to fill, plunged in nonetheless, thereby staking his claim as the "first person ever" to dive into the Tempe pool.

Before that people swam in the river, its waters so clean that they drank from it to quench their thirst and ate, according to Ray Chavarria, "what we called *vero* [*berro*]," thereby earning Tempe's Mexican residents the designation *comeberros*, (those who eat watercress). They dived from a springboard at "Point-in-the-Rocks," a large outcropping at the northeast corner of Tempe Butte, and gathered at a spot called Jointhead, some two and a half miles west of town, where Edward Curry recalls seeing on Sundays two or three thousand people swimming in the river.

Tempe's new alternative to river swims would be dug on land bought by Charles Hayden in 1870, then passed to C. A. Hooper in 1887 and later that year to the Tempe Land and Improvement Company, who sold it in 1920 to J. W. Kingsley (owner of Farmer's and Merchant's Bank). It was Normal School teacher Alva B. Clark, along with undertaker E. P. Carr and local doctor R. J. Stroud, who envisioned a park there, anchored by a pool where athletes could come to compete. When Kingsley then sold the land to the Tempe Civic Club for $1,900, he offered a rebate of $500 just for naming the spot Tempe Beach. In the end, the town of Tempe paid $1406.05 for the land, then raised an additional $3,000 to build the pool by selling stock in the project. This arrangement was a rousing success. Shareholders in the venture "not only got their money back, they received 4% interest on their funds by 1930."

Stories in the *Tempe Daily News* track the progress of this enterprise. In April an article points its readers to Garfield Goodwin's store where plans for the pool are on display. A month later another announces that construction has begun, Niels Stolberg having garnered the contract with a bid of $3200. By June, the paper tells us, the lot is being fenced; by July the pool is charging admission; by August its well contains eight feet of water, "sufficient for the needs of the pool."

Art Clark, son of Alva, remembers his father at about that time enlisting students in his wood-working class to build a "three-deck tower" at the pool. Also installed was a wooden bulkhead, so the somewhat too-long pool would conform to official swim-meet standards. In addition, the Normal School provided two cast-off wooden buildings which, fitted with wooden lockers, became men's and women's dressing rooms. At twelve Art himself served as Tempe Beach "key boy," wearing the master key around his neck to open those lockers for the pool's early patrons. He also remembers an octagonal structure made of river rocks that served as both office and ticket booth. On its roof lay mattresses where local boys would sometimes sleep, cooling off in the swimming pool during the night. The manager then was Eddie Scales, whose brother Harry, as the pool's sole lifeguard, "charmed the lady swimmers." By 1930 the seven-year average attendance at the pool totaled one hundred thousand swimmers per season.

View of pool showing octagonal structure at left

It is easy to see why the new Tempe Beach was such a draw. The pool itself measured 175 by 60 feet, its depth ranging from ten feet under the diving boards and twenty-five-foot tower to three and a half feet in the shallow end. A separate twenty-by-thirty foot children's pool lay to the east of the larger pool. Both were filled by a well whose motor pumped in water that was drained and replaced every several days. As one early patron testifies, "The water in this pool is always fresh and pure and always the right temperature." In addition, early on a cobble-stone bandstand and baseball field had been added to the site. Large cottonwoods stood in the grassy area beside the pool where people could picnic after they swam, with tamarisks planted at the edges of the park. This communal spot, as much as the pool itself, accounted for the pride people had in a place that became a kind of agora, the center of a small town's social life.

Joe Spracale, long-time swim coach and manager of Tempe Beach in the fifties, identifies the park's importance in just this way: "Everybody met here all the time; it was a meeting place of the whole community. As a fifteen-year old child you could come down here and sit under the big cottonwood trees, bring your lunch, whatever you liked, and people would just sit and meet, have a good time." Marvin Williams, life-long Tempean who coached the swim team in the sixties, echoes Joe's nostalgia for those early gatherings at Tempe Beach: "It was the big place to go in town, in Tempe, at the time. The town was very small—5,000 people—and what we would do, get a peanut butter sandwich, apple, maybe buy a candy bar on the way down to the pool, and stay there all day. And folks might drive by or come by to see if you were there."

Both men's descriptions of the pool in the forties call up writer Ray Oldenburg's concept of the "Third Place," a public space that is not home, but that engenders a feeling of "at homeness," a "freedom to be." "The Great Good Place," he tells us in his book by that name, offers easy and upbeat interactions and the comfort of its constancy: "At almost any time of the day or evening," one may go there alone "with assurance that acquaintances will be there." In the informality of its setting and the camaraderie it inspired, even decades later Tempe Beach was such a place.

In that first decade the pool became important as well for its role in furthering aquatic sports. One investor in the Tempe Beach project, Dr. Reginald James Stroud, had insisted that the pool conform to

Amateur Athletic Association standards so that records could be set there. As head of the Tempe Beach Committee, and by the 1930s AAU Commissioner for the state of Arizona, Stroud thus spearheaded a long tradition of holding meets at Tempe Beach.

On September 7, 1925—Labor Day—the new pool hosted its first official AAU swim meet. Two years later that annual meet became a hybrid: by day swimmers vied for medals; by night bathing beauties competed for the title of the state's first Miss Arizona. Although the pageant was moved from the pool to the capital the very next year, Tempe Beach will always be the site where the first-ever winner was crowned: Phoenix's entrant, Ethel Cole. At the 6th Annual AAU Swimming and Diving Championships, held at the Beach in 1930, swimmers and divers from as far away as Safford and Yuma joined contestants from Mesa, Tempe and Phoenix to compete in this all-day contest, with heats in the morning and finals in the evening under the lights.

By 1932 the pool had reached its zenith as a venue for water sports when it hosted what would be its most prestigious meet to date: the Women's National Swimming and Diving Championships, held just a few weeks after the Los Angeles-based Olympic Games. One article about this meet credits Dr. Stroud with an almost supernatural feat in bringing such a contest to small-town Tempe: "When you consider the fact that a town of 2,200 souls snatched a national championship meet from under the noses of such metropolitan centers as Cleveland and Seattle, the former with a population of nearly one million persons, you get some idea of just how miraculous the thing is." This article, titled "Praise for Dr. Stroud," then corrects such hyperbole by citing the simple power of place in determining the venue for a meet whose contestants were already gathered in near-by LA. Arranging their travel to Seattle or Cleveland—1500 and 2000 miles away respectively—would have been a more difficult task.

Still, it must have felt nothing short of divine to see world-class athletes in one's home-town pool. There, Eleanor Holm, recent winner of Olympic gold in the one-hundred meter backstroke, swam, while Dorothy Poynton (Olympic platform champion) and Katy Rawls (three-meter silver-medal winner) dived. Holm added to the citizens' thrill by breaking her world record right before their eyes while infusing the town with the glamour of her movie star good looks and her recently acquired film contract.

History, however, will not be kind to either Stroud or Holm, so lauded that week in the local press. Stroud will be forever known as a fierce defender of discrimination in excluding Mexicans from Tempe Beach. Holm will be kicked off the 1936 Olympic team for drinking champagne while en route to Berlin. (As Holm herself describes it, "This chaperone came up to me and said it was time to go to bed....So I said to her, "Oh, is it really bed time? Did you make the Olympic team or did I?") Those who watched her break that record four years earlier at Tempe Beach would certainly forgive her this display of hubris. Harder to forgive is Dr. Stroud's exclusion of certain citizens from Tempe Beach, his denying them access to this great, good place.

For forty more summers, until its closing in 1964, Tempe Beach will host competitions drawing talented swimmers from near and far. Though its tower will be gone, its diving tradition will continue too. Only three years after the Women's National Championship (where Katy Rawls beat Dorothy Poynton) local diver Dick Smith will take state high and low-board titles there, then go on to coach the likes of Patsy Willard and Bernie Wrightson, local Olympic-medal-winning divers, as well as the Beach's own lifeguard, Tempe's Chuck Holly. In the forties Lois Williams, sister of the lifeguard Marvin, will win State diving titles too, while in the fifties Jose Guaderrama will compete on the boards of Tempe Beach, then become, after Dan Arredondo, its second Mexican-American lifeguard. Although I don't know it in 1960, this long tradition will draw me too when in 1962, needing divers for his Tempe Beach Diving Team, Chuck will recruit me and my friend Daf. We will spend two summers on the very boards where champions once stood, neither of us able to remotely imagine the storied past of Tempe Beach.

Other Voices

Childhood at Tempe Beach
"Hey, there's that woman I bubble-bombed!"

Ramos Kids, circa 1954

By the time we discovered Tempe Beach, the waters had been drained and refilled hundreds of times, but for us, so young ourselves, the place felt new. My brothers, in fact, were in single digits when they swam here, unaccompanied by any parent, but protected by the surrogates, watching from the lifeguard stands. Jeff, the youngest, triggered alarms when he ventured past the shallow end. As he recalls: "I remember working on my breath-holding talents even when I was a little kid. When a lifeguard asked me to swim across the pool (the test you had to pass to be in the deep end) I said "sure" and proceeded to cross it under water. It made him scratch his head and rethink things."

Tom remembers being so young that he didn't feel bad "going over to the baby pool with the little kids" and so thin that a crucial challenge was keeping warm: "The technique I had to keep warm at Tempe Beach—ten years old, younger—was to lie on the sidewalk next to the pool with a little tiny towel over my shoulders, in a hot puddle of water. It was the only way to keep warm there."

I remember enlisting that poolside myself as a kind of middle-man between the frigid water and the towel that lay waiting far away on the lawn. Anyone who swam here as a child, back when everyone was lean, remembers cleaving to his towel and can feel Tom's pain one morning outside Tempe Beach:

"I remember once my dad drove me on his motor scooter and I was riding sitting on my towel, and I jumped off when we got to Tempe Beach, and off dad went, giving me my nickel or whatever it cost to get in, and I saw him driving off and I shouted and screamed because there on the back of his motor scooter was my towel, the only thing that lay between me and an icy, mammoth-like death. And so it just took the heart out of me, I remember. "

As much as we suffered from the cold of that water, its temperature could actually be an incentive in helping children learn to swim. It inspired Jim Settlemoir, for example, to persist in the final challenge of those early-summer lessons:

"Tempe Beach is where I took swimming lessons at the age of five. What I remember is that the water was FREEZING. Every chance we had we'd get out of the pool and lie on the cement to warm up. In order to

18

graduate you had to swim across the pool non-stop. I nearly drowned doing that, but there was NO WAY I was going to fail that final test and have to come back for another round of lessons."

The lifeguard-instructors must have understood that such suffering merited a fitting reward. After each round of lessons they held a party under the lights of Tempe Beach, throwing pennies in the pool for the graduates to gather and, at one point, devising an even more challenging way for the swimmers to showcase their skills. JoAnn (Voss) Brown recalls this pre-PETA evening of celebration at Tempe Beach: "Alex Arredondo was my swimming instructor that year. And at the end of the year at the party they held for all us graduates, they threw a bunch of gold fish in the pool for us to catch and take home." Though not all goldfish would survive their plunge into the pool that night, in its forty-year existence every child who swam there would. The combination of free swim lessons and attentive lifeguards made Tempe Beach a safe place to be.

With lessons over, the fun began, but that fun didn't happen of its own accord. Instead, it was allowed to flourish by the longstanding culture of the pool itself. There, guards sought not to assert their power but to minimize their need to do so. Alex Arredondo, lifeguard and manager, describes the method used by those in charge:

"Whatever [kids] wanted to do with their friends was okay as long as it wasn't illegal, and if somebody else tried to infringe on their area and they came up and complained, then we had to talk with that person. We'd pretty much supervise and talk to people—try to pick up their demeanor—and maybe that's why I went into education. I liked to talk to people and say, 'Hey, here's what we expect and here's what we're going to do. You okay with that?' And most of the time they were."

Of course such laissez-faire methods at times might result in a creative chaos ("They'd be trying to puncture someone's air-mattress. We'd be trying to save someone, and they'd be trying to drown someone"), but overall the lifeguard's mantra—a pre-Beatles version of "Let It Be"— ensured that fifty years later the mere mention of that pool will elicit a smile and a stream of happy memories.

Some of these involve behaviors that would be forbidden at any other pool. As Steve Cole recalls:

"[Tempe Beach] had a very relaxed and liberal dress code and swimsuit policy. You could swim in there in an inner tube; you could be wearing cut-off shorts; you could be wearing long pants and swim in there if you wanted to. I remember kids swimming with sweatshirts on, and once Tempe Beach became defunct and we went to the university pool, they had all kinds of strict regulations: bathing caps, you couldn't wear those California trunks (beachcombers); they'd throw you out."

Those sweatshirts, for the most part, were a high-board hedge against the belly-flop, a kind of insurance when attempting new dives. At times, however, they would double as towels, as mats, or even as equipment in poolside play. As Mary Jane (Wegner) Torok remembers: "Once I had a wet sweatshirt, and so I spun it around and then I was jump-roping with it. I caught my foot and fell flat on my face. And you guys laughed at me. I was so humiliated...because I was probably showing off, you know, was going to do a little jump-roping and— SPLAT!"

Sweatshirts, cutoffs, and uncapped hair were hardly a problem in a fill-and-drain pool. Flotation devices were another story, creating as they did both occasions for horseplay and barriers to vision. That they were allowed at the Beach at all is a testament to the lifeguards' focus not on the ease of their own surveillance but on the assurance that Tempe's children would have a good time.

Underwater gear was welcome too: "We'd bring a mask and snorkel," Tom remembers, though bringing such attractions to a pool filled with children might provide a lesson no instructor could teach:

"Once there was a brother and sister, I believe; they seemed to be country yokels or something. They'd never seen a mask and snorkel, and they kept borrowing mine. They were pushy, kept taking them for 'just another half-hour.' I didn't want them having them, but I couldn't say no to these poor hayseeds and off they went with them, and it was kind of the first time I noticed that I didn't have, you know, I wasn't assertive enough with my stuff. I do remember that."

The lifeguards' tolerance also gave children, with or without stuff, the freedom to create their own fun, as did my brother Jeff and his friend John Wood, in inventing the infamous bubble-bomb. The young pranksters' merriment still survives in the very description of this long-ago stunt:

"With lungs full you would cruise the very bottom of the ten-foot end. On your back you would station yourself under the secured ladder where people got out of the pool. There was an art to squeezing your nose and cupping your hand around your mouth, aiming a huge exhalation of air in the form of a basketball-sized bubble that would ascend to the person's butt. It almost always caused an *'Ooh! Eeh!'* We spent hours at that ridiculous activity. John and I were damn good at it. 'Hey, there's that woman I bubble-bombed!' Bubble-bombing each other was usually a sneak attack."

Other pastimes involved a similar management of air. As today's youth might measure their status by the level they'd achieved in a video game, we gauged ours in pool widths, or even lengths, always attempting—lungs on fire—to push on still farther before drawing a breath. Laure (Wegner) Kagen reminded me that one requirement for our Water Badge was to swim the pool's width under water. Swim coach Marvin recalls those early mornings with the pool newly filled: "Beautiful. I loved that. I'd try to hold my breath and swim the whole length." He remembers a swim team member being able to "do it once and then back again," an amazing feat with only two opportunities to push off the wall, but David Link (THS Class of '68) corroborates this memory: "I think what I remember most [about Tempe Beach] was nearly everyone trying to swim the length of the pool underwater. If I remember correctly, a number of kids could go up and back."

Donna Wells consulted an ex-swimmer friend to check the accuracy of these claims: "His slow time under water in a twenty-five yard pool was forty seconds per lap. So if the TB pool was fifty yards, two laps could have been done in under three minutes without a breath—doable for a conditioned swimmer." Gerry Turley concurs: "In college as a conditioned football lineman I could swim the Olympic size pool width four times under water. But that was with push offs. I was also 280 pounds, so I assume someone smaller than me could have done much more."

A simpler method of gauging one's prowess dispensed with the need to swim at all as one merely slipped beneath the surface and ticked off seconds instead of pool widths: "I remember staying underwater for ridiculous counts," Jeff told me. But hard to beat in time logged under water is Coach Dick Smith, whose boasting made its way into print: "[Smith] claimed to be able to hold his breath for four minutes; a minor vanity, and an unusual one for a man of fifty-seven, but he was no ordinary American in late middle age. He had devoted his whole life to sport, had coached the US Olympic diving teams in 1964 and 1968, and ran his own swimming gymnasium in Phoenix, Arizona." Still, Tom Ditsworth witnessed someone top even that: "One of U of A's swimmers (when I was at U of A) held his breath for four and a half minutes while a bunch of us watched. He hyperventilated for several minutes before lying down in bed and going into complete relaxation mode."

Less geared toward fame in our underwater exploits, we girls amused ourselves with a game we called Bobbing: a Zen-like emptying out of all our air as we sank to the bottom, a push back up to the surface from that ten-foot depth, and a blissful replenishment, our bodies, like the pool itself, drained then filled. I remember the quiet of those plunges, the noise of the jukebox and cannonballs left high above as we descended in an envelope of bubbles until even that sound vanished and, lungs emptied out, we made our ascent. In the midst of the fray, we must have needed this periodic sorting out, these deep retreats, as the young boys needed their underwater pranks and the older boys their bragging rights. We fulfilled these needs using what we had in full supply: water and breath. Back then boys and girls alike could pull a summer's amusement out of thin air.

Amid all these deep-water games lay the pool's few ready-made methods of play: the boys' games of Dare Base, Sharks and Fishes, and Corner Tag, and that long-established game learned by all who swam in the ten-foot end. Dibble-dabble was universal in its appeal: simple and mildly competitive, a variation on the classic "Fetch," in that she who "tossed out" might also retrieve. If the clarity of first-day water made the game too easy, one could ramp up the challenge by breaking the popsicle stick in half or even into quarters, as Tom remembers doing. In a more elaborate modification, Jeff would take down a handful of sticks in a version that evolved over time:

"Multiple dibble-dabble started one day when we collected a lot of sticks. At first we just went down and let a lot go. Then, I don't know if it was Emmett or Jan or Scott (or even me) who thought of writing numbers on them. One guy would dive down and then whoever was the caller would yell a number and then everyone would see if the stick they found had that number."

Joanie (Johnson) Hartman recalls simply waiting for the water itself to make more sporting the search for the stick: "I loved the pool when it was clean and clear; however dibble-dabble was more fun when the pool was a little murky. It made the hunt more challenging." Linda (Carnal) Whatley remembers tokens of this game being left on her body—"having a constant bruise on my knees from climbing out of the pool all day long"—as well as moments when the hunters in this simple game would become themselves the hunted: "Stanley Rogers used to chase all the girls in the pool, catch them, dunk them, and take the rubber bands from pony tails. I think it was like a notch in his belt that by the end of the day he counted rubber bands."

Hair itself, when freed from those bands, never failed to amuse. Leaning forward in the pool, we would dunk our heads, then resurface with a sleek, wet curtain of hair obscuring our view. With a simple motion we would flip it back into a roll, a kind of reverse breaking wave, then laugh uproariously at the effect. Though no one would have seen it then, with our rigid updos we were reminiscent of the FLDS, minus the piety and prairie dress.

Hair Play

25

Boys manipulated their hair too, even pre-Fab Four, their cuts just long enough to need, on occasion, a hands-free primp. I can still see boys resurfacing from high-board dives and, almost before taking a breath, flicking their hair with a twist of their necks to restore its loft, or swimming with it flying from side to side in a stroke reminiscent of the two-tiered town that Tempe had been not that long ago. As Tom describes it: "More often than not the kids had had lessons. They'd do a left turn with their heads for a gasp of air. But others would thrash their head from side to side like Johnny Weissmuller, and the hair would fly. This is the way you'd swim in the canals."

These memories, stored like snapshots in some deep mind-vault, lie ready to surface, even after fifty years, along with the remnants of sound or smell still lingering after all that time. I'd completely forgotten until several people dredged it up, the turnstile exit to Tempe Beach: "I still remember the constant creaking all day of that thing turning every time someone left (Linda)." "I remember the exit gate that spun. We would climb up and ride it like a merry-go-round (Joanie)." "I remember a girl got her foot caught on a bolt on that revolving gate, and when they got her loose she made bloody footprints (Steve)." I'd forgotten too the lost towels, hung on the fence by grounds man Phil Acosta, the bikes Doug Royse remembers seeing—"approximately two hundred in the bike parking area and none that I noted were locked"— the grill around the drain in the deep end that resembled, according to Charlene (Mills) Ashworth, the front of a train. Elissa (Montgomery) Tap recalls a waterfall feature in the kiddie pool, the sensation of it washing over her body, and, less happily, those times when a baby's accident would force the children from the pool as a lifeguard drained it and hosed it out.

Others recollect the colors of those days, the "white zinc oxide on our noses (Linda)"; the swim-team ribbons, "a lot of yellow, green and purple as I recall (Tom Ditsworth)"; the lifeguards' swim trunks, "so red in June but ... sun-bleached light red by August (Doug)"; the tan of our bodies: "I used to brown up so brown, a deep mahogany brown, and people used to come up to me and say, 'I've never seen anyone who had a suntan as dark as you (Steve)'"; or the pink: "After a summer of marinating in highly chlorinated pool water and walking home in the desert sun, my blonde hair was bleached bone white and my eyes were perpetually pink. I looked like the offspring of a human parent and the Easter Bunny" (Steve Hancock).

Still others remember smells: "The girls' locker/ shower room was always steamy and musty. You had to pass through the locker room (theoretically to take a shower before getting in the pool) so we would walk really fast just to get out of there (Linda)." "The smell of the hot dogs (Mary Jane)." "I remember the smell of bubble gum and of course the chlorine and lying in that warm puddle of water. I remember how that smelled (Tom)." And the related faculty, taste: "What did we call that awful "taffy" shit? I can still taste it, unfortunately (Jeff)."

With only a few exceptions, everyone recalls the sounds of the jukebox, dating themselves by the songs they name: "The jukebox was there. I remember under the veranda there, the ramada out back next to the snack bar, and they would play that jukebox: 'Scream, scream, put another dime in the record machine.' They were dancing out there to this. 'Shout, shout, knock yourself out.' That's the song I remember (Tom)." My sister Wendy cites "Walk Don't Run" as the tune she associates with Tempe Beach, while Dan Arredondo, who managed the snack bar, names "Itsy Bitsy Teeny-Weeny Yellow Polka-dot Bikini." For Mary Jane it was "Cathy's Clown": "Every time I hear it I'm right back up there on the high dive." Other often-mentioned tunes include "Wolverton Mountain," "Will You Still Love Me Tomorrow," "Twist and Shout," "Purple People Eater," and "Sealed With a Kiss."

Most surprising to me was the song Joe Spracale loved and still remembers playing on the jukebox at Tempe Beach: Nat King Cole's "Nature Boy." Although every long-imprinted song inspires a yearning for those childhood days, "Nature Boy" in its very lyrics calls up the magic of a golden age: Tempe Beach in the forties. In this 1947 hit, Cole sings of a magical time, when an enchanted boy "passed my way." The song is haunting, wistful. To imagine it wafting from the jukebox at Tempe Beach is to somehow know that we missed out on this golden age—we who swam there later. "You were right on the end of it," Chuck (Holly) told me. "You won't find as many people in their 70s or 80s [who remember the forties at Tempe Beach]. You'll find more of us. Well, I'm 68. You'll find us, and we're the ones that dream about this wonderful time."

The swimming-pool dream anticipates the future as well as recalling an idyllic past. It is an ideal vision projected forward, a wish for connection across generations and beyond time. Writer James Dickey had a recurrent swimming pool dream in which his closest friends were sitting at the poolside, chatting. As Dickey's son describes it: "There was nothing special about the pool itself. No one walked on water. And he never told me who the friends were. But what he took away from the dream was a sense of contentment, of being at ease with himself and the world as if he had gotten a preview of heaven. He called that place 'The Happy Swimming Pool.'" So apt a descriptor is Dickey's phrase that I almost chose it as the title for this book. Tempe Beach was a happy swimming pool, a joyfully remembered place.

Getting to Tempe Beach
"Bullheads are invincible"

To value the journey above the destination is a lesson we have all been taught. And so it is no surprise that when asked for their memories of Tempe Beach people will, inevitably, end up recounting the voyage there: across burning pavement and railroad tracks, along well-known streets— College, Tenth, Thirteenth, Farmer—through the ASU campus, past the storefronts on the west side of Mill, riding bikes and walking, running from shady spot to shady spot or up onto grass with feet on fire: "Bare feet wasn't something we suffered with; it was a preference, the way it should be" (Jeff). On the way there we brimmed with anticipation. On the way back we ached with hunger. Not surprisingly the home-bound tales fairly drip with grease.

Harry Mitchell came from the west-side, setting out from Roosevelt Street with his dog, a Labrador Retriever, following behind. The dog, loving water, would run through the bathhouse and leap into the baby pool, eliciting shrieks from the mothers sitting there until the loud speaker blared out the order that he get his dog and take it home. Linda (Carnal) Whatley also came from the west, riding with friends on bikes along

13th Street over to Farmers Avenue, then straight up Farmers to 1st Street and Tempe Beach:

"Of course there was no traffic, so that wasn't even an issue. One year my dad bought a tandem bike for our family and so I would then recruit someone to ride the tandem with me—usually Cathy Scarborough (who later died when we were in high school) or Valerie McMillion, who were neighbors and buddies at the time."

Nancy (Leach) Lesko walked from her Daley Park house just north of Broadway "barefoot to Tempe Beach because those were the days before flip flops and athletic shoes." Although we often took the route around Daley Park to College as well, Wendy Cole remembers walking west on Broadway to Mill and then turning north: "We used to go under the underpass on Mill Avenue by the high school; it was cool in there in the shade and by the Dairy Queen. I remember all the carvings on the picnic tables. We always walked and we never wore shoes." Charlene (Mills) Ashworth would sometimes pause at the corral on her way down Maple or Ash and "try to get an "EE-HAH" out of Jericho the donkey." Jeff Cole often went with Emmett Aepli, varying their route. "Once we took the tracks from Daley Park to the overpass at Mill by the high school." When by himself, though, Jeff would run:

"I used to think my first flirting with distance running was at Lake Itasca when I ran to the swimming beach daily to assist Bill Underhill, who paid me a bit for it, but now that I think of it, on my lone jaunts to Tempe Beach I used to jog on my toes for most of the way. Was it to minimize the time my feet were exposed to the burning pavement?"

Tom remembers running only once:

"Bobby Valdez and I decided to run from his house clean to Tempe Beach. And we ran barefoot. We never wore shoes. We'd jump to the grass so we didn't burn our feet right off. We didn't stop the whole way, and went swimming. And the next day (we didn't know what the effects would be of such a fast run without any building up to it or training), neither one of us, for the first few minutes of the day, we couldn't really walk. Our legs were just too ruined from this. And Bobby told me how he had gotten out of bed in the morning. He said, 'I just flipped those covers aside and jumped out—and fell on my face.' My God, it was two miles, maybe two and a half, which doesn't sound like very far away, but when you're running in the sun—you'd never have a ride. That's why we didn't have an ounce of fat on us."

The thread that links the walkers and the runners in these tales is their common struggle with cement and asphalt stoked by desert sun, a sun so hot that we'd be forced to jump onto our towels, or into a shady spot, or onto the street ("The white painted lines in the middle of the street were about five degrees cooler-big relief for the feet") or even, in desperation, onto someone's lawn: out of the frying pan into the briar. The bullheads in those yards were to the Tempean what the Great White is to the Australian, a tier-one predator, destroying even children with feet so calloused that ordinary stickers didn't faze them ("those stickers would just collect on our feet until we decided to scrape them off"), feet so calloused that heat barely registered: "John Wood once stomped out a lit cigarette with his bare foot somewhere around where Monti's still is" (Jeff).

Not only was the bullhead multi-pronged, thus resembling a two-horned bull, each prong had the strength of titanium. Bike tires succumbed to it: "All the kids knew that you NEVER bought regular gauge tires for your bike. Only HEAVY DUTY. Heavy duties could withstand bullheads that got through the tires, but regular tubes would only last one day" (Tom). Jim Settlemoir, however, puts his money on the bullhead every time: "Bullheads are invincible. I've had them puncture knobby mountain bike tires that had heavy duty tubes."

One never forgets a bullhead encounter, whether on the way to the pool or not. Ruth Corson remembers them in the park: "We all got bused to Daley Park in the summer for watermelon and water balloon fights, and of course we were ALL barefoot (sigh). Full of HUGE bullheads. We were all bleeding when we got through." But my favorite bullhead story, by Katharine Karyszyn (FKA Deborah Hood), could pass for an episode of Lassie:

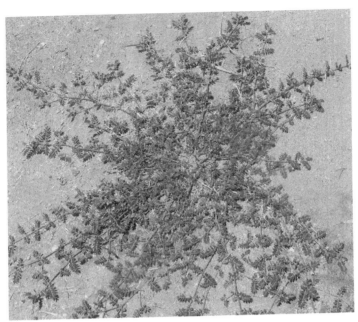

Bullhead Sticker Patch

"When my brother vanished for a day when he was about nine, he walked to our grandparents' house in Phoenix (about eleven miles away) and our dog Dinah went with him. At some point he took off his shoes and tied them to her collar, then couldn't get them untied. So when he came to a huge area of bullheads he had to ride Dinah through them. What a great dog!"

Though painful, bullhead encounters were part of the process of getting to Tempe Beach, and thus embraced as a minor glitch in a journey otherwise distinguished by the high it afforded us: the sheer exhilaration of being young and on our own with a whole town to navigate, a sun-drenched place rife with spots made for lingering until at last all roads led to merchants' row, at the end of which lay Tempe Beach.

Jeff recalls the warm-up pranks he would pause for some half way to the swimming pool:

"Sometimes we would cut through the ASU campus to fool around. We had ways of rigging the vending machines. Most were techniques devised by Jan Bradbury who never saw a contraption he couldn't master from kites to bikes to German Taunuses. So we could get six or seven chocolate milks for a quarter instead of one or jam the spout in the coke machine so we could fill up until it came out mostly soda water. Of course there was no real use in having so many milks or so much coke, but it was an activity that gave us the warm, proactive feeling of having gotten away with something."

Steve Hancock catalogues his stops along Mill in what has become a kind of cult classic, the ten-page memoir "A Trip to Tempe Beach." In it he names each establishment on either side of Mill, from the Tempe Woman's Club on the northwest corner of Mill and 13th Street to Monti's on 1st Street, just across from Tempe Beach. He would bike or walk from his house on 14th Street with his brother Bill "or some neighborhood pal" and, like Jeff, might stop along the way, maybe at Miller's Indian Store, drawn in by an object in their window display: "a taxidermy concoction whereby a monkey's head and shoulders had been married to the body of a large fish. The taxidermy skills that put this thing together were first rate and enhanced by an overall patina of dust and grime that gave it an appearance of authenticity and antiquity. It was a small-boy magnet."

Indian Store in Tempe

It would be a mistake, however, to imply that no one was driven to Tempe Beach. Those who lived in neighboring towns would, of course, come by car. Sharon Southerland and her east-Mesa family would set out once a year as a special occasion to swim and picnic in the park. Coming over the bridge she remembers seeing a billboard with an ocean scene and thinking she was going to an actual beach.

Many locals, as well, arrived by car. In fact, Alex recalls a standard drop-off and pick-up pattern: "It was a time when parents would bring their kids down at like ten in the morning and then see them at four o'clock. You didn't have to look at the clock. You could tell it was four." Even my working mother would sometimes come by to pick us up. I remember not the ride itself but the humiliation of the loudspeaker blaring over Tempe Beach: "Cole children. Your mother is waiting for you at the bathhouse."

That disembodied voice belonged, at least most of the time, to Millie Loughrige, the synchronized swim coach who worked in the bath house: taking our baskets, handing us an "extra large safety pin with our basket number," and announcing on the PA that our parents were waiting to take us home. Even after all these years ("though I wouldn't know her if I saw her now") one name still echoes in Millie's mind, that of Penelope du Chantelet: "I always thought that was so beautiful. And I used to try to get to the microphone before anybody else."

Tom recalls Millie's voice broadcasting his less lyrical name, and that of his friend John Wood, on those rare occasions when some parent would save them the long walk home:

"One day we got a ride home from Tempe Beach, which was unusual. It was Bill Wood who drove us back. He drove me and John; he might have done it more than once because I remember one time I threw a candy wrapper out the window of the car. It wasn't very green of me, but he stopped the car and went back and picked it up, said, 'You know, I don't like trash being thrown in my town.' So anyway I learned my lesson. One day I got in the car and I said, 'Oh, no, I left my shirt at Tempe Beach!' A white tee shirt, and Bill Wood pulled into Joe Sellah's Sporting Goods or somewhere, one of those stores on Mill Avenue, and said, 'Wait, boys.' And about three minutes later he came back. He had bought me a new tee shirt. All the guys were amazed: 'He bought you a new tee shirt!' It was bright white, you know, so it's kind of an interesting memory. Bill Wood."

Most often, however, we returned from the swimming pool the way we had come, on bikes or by foot, stopping not for amusement but for food. Although the snack bar at the pool could have sustained us, we patronized the businesses on Mill instead, perhaps because of the era's advisement that to swim after eating was to risk cramping up and drowning within sight of shore. As Linda remembers: "Cathy Scarborough's mom was a waitress at Monti's. We were really lucky because we could go over to Monti's with Cathy and get a free hamburger, which was a real treat. After lunch (and waiting an hour for our food to digest!) we would return to the pool for the afternoon."

Few of us would have had the discipline to sit out that hour by the poolside at Tempe Beach, so we refueled our bodies on the long walk home while quenching our thirst, perhaps, at Mark Bailey's pick for the "coldest water fountain in town": the one at Nevitt's Richfield station on the southwest corner of 7th Street and Mill. Buddy Davis recalls hitting up his dad for thirty cents on summer mornings, "fifteen to get in to the pool and fifteen to spend at Pete's Fish and Chips for a plate full of French fries on the way home." Doug Royse remembers riding his bike down to Tempe Beach two or three times weekly with that same return plan: "on the way home for a quarter buying a large plate of French fries and a coke—so filling." Charlene Ashworth would stop at Pete's too, buying for a nickel a piece of fish, while Chuck recalls stopping at a bakery on Mill: "Our favorite stop was the Dutch Oven Bakery. They always had day-old goodies at half price. My favorite was potato rolls with the white flour dusted on top." Eldon Smith would buy there a kind of sugar cookie, "the size of a small pizza" for his post-swimming treat. Steve Hancock patronized the Dutch Oven too, calling it the "third in a troika of places where...we could choose to feed ourselves," the other two being Pete's Fish and Chips and the Dairy Queen. The treat he would choose sounds strangely like Eldon's:

"The big draw at the Dutch Oven was the Pecan Crispy, a flat, saucer-like cookie about eight inches in diameter that was made from thin layers of dough baked with cinnamon and crushed pecans on top. You could walk five or six blocks before crunching the entire thing down, leaving a moraine of flaky crumbs on the front of your t-shirt."

Many of us waited until 10th Street and the third in Hancock's troika, the Dairy Queen, where for a nickel we could buy a cone, one dipped in chocolate for a dime or, when flush with cash, a sundae or milkshake for fifty cents. So far into caloric debt were we that no grease or milk-laced snack could ruin the dinners we were heading toward, those mandated sit-down affairs with parents and children at the end of the day. And so we ate as we walked or rode our bikes, one hand on the handlebars, the other clutching a dwindling snack: French fries, milkshake, potato roll.

To this day the mere sight of a Dairy Queen can call up four o'clock/generic summer/Tempe, Arizona, where a slow procession is taking place, a reversal of those earlier forays cross- town to the swimming pool: The calorie-depleted and the newly refueled are making their way home from Tempe Beach, through familiar streets—Farmer, Thirteenth, Tenth, College—or along the tracks, pedaling or walking (no one running), everyone sun-turned—pink or mahogany—bearing bruises and bullhead stigmata, everyone spent from a day at Tempe Beach.

Tenth and Mill

Second-Day Water

Memoir

The next summer, the summer of '61, I wore a suit still prominent in my own private Beachwear Hall of Fame, not because it was particularly memorable for its color or charm but because it marked my first venture into the world of the two-piece. In a fitting sound-track to my debut in this suit, a top-choice jukebox song that year was "Itsy-Bitsy, Teeny-Weeny, Yellow Polka-dot Bikini." And so as I sat in the bathhouse that opening day, reliving one of my worst "going to school in your underwear" nightmares, I replayed in my mind its apt first verse with refrain:

> She was afraid to come out of the bathhouse
> She was as nervous as she could be
> She was afraid to come out of the bathhouse
> She was afraid that somebody would see
> Two, three, four, tell the people what she wore
>
> It was an itsy, bitsy, teenie, weenie, yellow polka-dot bikini
> That she wore for the first time today
> An itsy, bitsy, teenie, weenie, yellow polka-dot bikini
> So in the bathhouse she wanted to stay.

Like the girl in the song, I lingered. In a burst of courage, I'd walk to the exit and then, on second thought, would beat a quick retreat. For what seemed like a lifetime I sat there conflicted, the sounds of the cannonballs luring me outward, my modesty inevitably drawing me back. Eventually the water won out and I emerged in my hardly scanty bathing suit. It was blue with little-boy legs and a high-cut top so that only a few-inch strip of mid-drift distinguished it from last year's one-piece. But this was still a fifties-sitcom world into which I had been thoroughly socialized. I wanted my mother, who had two swimsuits—one she referred to as her "faculty wife suit" and the other a bona fide bikini—to be June Cleaver, not the unconventional woman she was.

I still remember the day when Laure and a classmate named Barbara came home with me after school. My mother wasn't home, so we tried next door where sure enough we found her, stretched out on a chaise-lounge next to our neighbor, both of them in tiny bikinis, cigarettes in their hands, ample cleavage popping from their tops. It was as shocking as the day when Laure and I, babysitting in that same house, found the husband's stash of *Playboys*. My eyes welled up as we returned to my house, and Laure—noticing this—said, "When I grow up, I'm going to wear a bikini," a remark for which to this day I could kiss her.

Only four years later I will be buying my own bikinis and wearing them to jump off cliffs at Canyon Lake. My father will say, on noting my purchases, "A lot of money for so little fabric." But now, the summer of '61, I'm a stranger to my body. It surprises me, especially when I stand up after lying on the pool-deck to see the imprint I've left, hipbones and incipient breasts, which I erase with a hasty splash of water.

That summer and the next two, I remember being often with Daf, who lived just across Broadway on my same street, Sierra Vista. My sister Wendy and Laure's sister Mary Jane, just two years older than we and already full-fledged teens, would sit on towels by the pool side, hair in lacquered bubbles, posing for the lifeguards. This was an opportunity not to be missed.

Daf and I would stick our hair in the pool, run over to them, and shake it out as they screamed in phony protest, actually grateful for the eyes drawn toward them.

Our motives were less clear. On the one hand such playfulness masked a strain of hostility. That summer I had a school-girl's crush on the lifeguard Alex, and these two were stiff competition. On the other hand their stasis and inhibition loomed as a grim reminder where Daf and I were headed: away from this glorious freedom into a gender-circumscribed world. Our wet-dog shake could be seen as a kind of rebellion against what the world had in store for us.

In fact, that whole summer I remember behaving in a childish way that belied the messages my body was sending. Daf and I spent a lot of time doing dramatic belly-flops from the pool's edge, then swimming out and back to the poolside in a flat-out worst crawl ever, our arms flailing, our butts sticking out of the water. We'd also mimic the synchronized swimming moves the older girls were perfecting at their morning practice. Our favorite move involved sculling under water while turning in a circle, our knees drawn up into a seated position, our form in every way exemplary, except that our toes, instead of being pointed, would be splayed, a half-inch of air separating each digit. All summer long we played out our conflicts in the cloudy waters of Tempe Beach, rejecting all things feminine—grace, beauty, and decorum—while at the same time seeking to draw the male gaze: those shaded eyes perpetually watching from the lifeguard stands around the pool.

In the meantime, the high board drew us, the city's tweens, as well as older boys whose cutoffs and sweatshirts would buffer their landings, those booming entries with knees drawn up to form the "cannon" ball or— with one leg pulled to the chest, the body angled backward—the more graceful "figure four." The pay-off for each dive lay in its finish, that high jet of water that rose from the perfect confluence of leg position, heft and entry angle. Sometimes the resulting spray would shoot so high that the boy would surface to the ultimate reward: a shower raining down on his head. When this occurred pool rules were suspended as instead of getting out of the way the boy would bask in his success— lingering till the spray ran out—while all eyes turned to admire his feat.

We girls became adept at the figure four ourselves, though we never managed to break the surface in time to meet the splash we'd made. At some point I remember Laure teaching us the sit-dive, a kind of gateway plunge that laid the groundwork for the scarier standing and springing dives. From a sitting position at the end of the board she'd roll backwards, knees bent, back flat against the board and then roll forward, her momentum carrying her off the end head-first into the pool. The beauty of this dive was that sitting down obscured one's view of that ten-foot chasm between board and pool until the forward roll would render futile any last-ditch notion of backing down. At some point Daf and I moved on to the handstand. We'd walk to the end of the board, stand on our hands, and then, as we started to tip, push off from the board to enter head-first or, alternatively, arch our backs to come full circle and enter feet-first, our arms raised over our heads.

I remember once an adult infiltrated the high-board line, executing fancy flips and offering judgments on our free-wheeling play. As I finished a dive and swam to the ladder, a group of girls met me to report, "That guy said you'd be a good diver if you'd just point your toes." For the rest of the afternoon I did my handstands with legs apart, toes splayed, in a firm rejection of even the slightest prescription from the grown-up world. For this was our place— this long, deep pool ringed with lifeguard stands—our own creation. We invented its games, dives, strokes and ground rules; we invented ourselves here, answering only to the lifeguard's tweet.

I remember most fondly jumping off the high board into second-day water, its hue only slightly blue, its temperature congenial, since it carried the tally of yesterday's sun. I remember the hours spent poised on the ladder overlooking that water, counting off the rungs as I waited my turn. I wish I had been there to rescue it out of the rubble when they tore down the pool: that ladder whose steps had once held Tempe's children, countless generations who had waited with their fears and their aspirations, every rung having borne that weight.

History

1933-1943
The Second Decade of Tempe Beach

Bath House 1934

Shortly after the Women's National Swimming and Diving Meet in 1932, Tempe Beach underwent a series of improvements to its site. The first of these was a new stone bathhouse to replace the two original 25 x 30 foot wooden structures where the beach's first swimmers had bought their passes—fifteen cents for adults, ten cents for children—and rented their towels for an extra nickel (for three extra nickels, even their suits). Private funding by the Tempe Woman's Club, the Tempe Rotary Club, the Tempe Fireman's Association and the Tempe Cemetery Committee allowed work to begin on this 100 x 300 foot river-rock structure, but clever thinking by the Tempe Beach Committee assured its completion with WPA funds. Having learned that the government

51

preferred funding projects already begun, the members put up two thousand dollars and began the addition of a playground adjacent to the swimming pool. By doing so they garnered twenty-seven thousand dollars in government funds, which resulted in not only a finished bathhouse but "a small concrete trough around the edge of the pool to improve sanitation," and a 2.7-acre park, complete with softball fields and tennis courts, a three-lane bowling alley, areas for shuffleboard, croquet and horseshoes, and a river-rock grandstand, whose ruins still exist today as do portions of the river-rock fence that formed the perimeter of the site.

For a single summer in 1934, the year the new bathhouse opened its doors, the park even boasted a movie screen, erected by Tempe's Dwight "Red" Harkins, who would also build the College Theater (later named the Valley Art) as well as an empire bearing his name. When we were ten or eleven, Laure and I got caught up in the messy transition of this all-ages theater into an art house as, following the movie we had come to see, a second feature, decidedly adult, appeared on the screen. Five "branded" women, heads shaved, one of them obviously pregnant, skinny dipped as a crucial plot thread dawned upon us: the women had been fraternizing with German soldiers during World War Two, which explained that pregnancy as well as the stubble. In a world where even bikinis were shocking, where a friend's mother scolded her for saying "pregnant" instead of using the coded "PG," Laure and I were understandably shaken as we walked up the aisle and out into the sun.

Early Harkins' Theater

Red Harkins' Tempe Beach venture had as many glitches as this art-house transition. Just as someone had forgotten about the two ten-year-olds in the theater, Harkins forgot about the monsoon in planning his open-air venture. As a result, dust storms and rain cut short some showings and a fierce storm late in the summer tore up the screen and damaged the projector room as water pooled on the floor he'd constructed without a drain. The whole endeavor lasted three short months.

As much a success as the Harkins theater was a failure, the tennis courts flourished. By 1936 tournament play had begun on them while in 1937, when lights were installed on the softball fields, night games began there for Tempe, Phoenix, and Mesa teams. Until the early sixties, American Legion baseball teams used the soft-ball dimensioned diamond. There was even a women's league and a team of Mexican-American players called "The Latin Americans." Local TV star Ladmo coached Little League teams there: Pee

Wees (six to seven year olds), Rookies (eight and nine year olds) and the Ladmo All-Stars. Today, men my age and somewhat older feel the same nostalgia for that softball field that I do for the swimming pool. For several generations of Tempeans, that plot was their great, good place.

In 1937 the town had its chance to showcase these changes to the pool and playground when it staged another national competition, one that, the official program claims, would "surpass in both number of competitors and spectators" the 1932 women's meet. "For you who are not acquainted with the nature of the event," the program continues, it is "to swimming what a national track meet containing such stars as Glen Cunningham, Ben Eastman, Jessie Owens, Bill Sefton and the like would be to that sport." As the earlier meet drew medalists from the Los Angeles based Olympic Games, this meet—The National AAU Far Western Swimming and Diving Championships—attracted those who had foregone the ship's champagne to arrive in Berlin just a year before still members of the Olympic team. Conspicuously absent from the program is Eleanor Holm Jarret. Instead, the new national backstroke champion Billie Steitz appears there, billed as the 1936 Olympian who recently came "within six seconds of the world record set by Miss Jarret at Tempe in 1932." Two Olympic ten-foot divers are mentioned as well, Katherine Rawls, who had beaten Dorothy Poynton at Tempe Beach five years before, and fourteen year old Marjorie Gestring, who had edged out the heavily favored Rawls by a half a point in Berlin to earn her portrayal here as "perhaps the finest diver in the world today."

Filling in for Holm in the glamour department are Ruth Nurmi, the National Junior ten-foot diving champion who "has had many movie offers," and the twins Marian and Virginia Hopkins, whose synchronized swimming routine—the Water Waltz—is claimed here to be "the only one of its kind in existence." The program describes the event as "two women in the water going through the movements of the aquatic dance with ease and grace." Soon, such novelty routines will become officially sport when the first US competition in synchronized swimming is held at Wright Junior College in Illinois on May 27, 1939. There, the swimmers will be judged not only on their grace but on their strength, endurance, timing, and breath control, a refreshing change from the tendency of the local papers to pose Olympic champions in the stances of beauty queens, to point out the blondness of Dorothy Poynton, and even to characterize world-class swimmer Holm as a woman "who has gained fame as an exponent of pulchritude as well as the aquatic arts."

Both this program and the newspaper articles about the meet make it seem an exclusively female affair, so downplayed is the presence of the male events. The *Phoenix Gazette*, for example, ran full-body photos of the female stars accompanied by a salacious text: "If you haven't noticed that female athletes are becoming easier on the eye year by year as well as better in competition, you have only to visit the south-side pool tonight, Saturday and Sunday nights. As an example, the pictures printed on this page will give you an idea of what you've been missing. Shapely lassies, aren't they?"

A highly featured event, however, is advertised as pure sports drama: the pitting of Katherine Rawls against Iris Cummings in a kind of aquatic throw-down to settle once and for all a hotly debated question of rank: The two women's times "are approximately the same in many events and the superiority of either of them in a medley event which mixes the strokes has never been definitively settled." The contest, however, seems not to have taken place. Instead, the papers report on a different event where "Katherine Rawls, one of the world's outstanding aquatic performers, was defeated in a 150-meter medley race against three state stars, each of whom swam fifty meters in their respective specialties." The outcome of this event is hardly surprising, since Rawls swam three times the distance of the others and was disadvantaged by the early start of the final swimmer, who began when Rawls touched the wall instead of waiting for her teammate.

Fifteen years later, swimmers entering a medley event will master four instead of three separate strokes as the butterfly, originally considered an offshoot of the breast stroke, will gain acceptance as a separate event. Henceforth at their morning practices, medley swimmers on the Tempe Beach team will train for this more challenging course, while at their earlier practice the city's girls will learn an updated version of the Water Waltz from their synchronized swim coach. Though journalists will no longer fixate on the "pulchritude" of these female athletes, the girls will themselves have internalized that message. Rather than recalling their coach's skill, they will remember her beauty: "Our coach Millie Loughrige was a young, pretty lady with very long blonde hair, and all of us wanted to look just like Millie." In a wholly predictable counter-reaction, Daf and I will spend our summer poking fun at the female ideal, spinning— toes widespread—beneath the lifeguard stands, "two [not quite] women in the water going through the movements of the aquatic dance with [anything but] ease and grace," two girls at the outset of womanhood testing the waters at Tempe Beach.

No Mexicans Allowed

Although Tempe Beach history is filled with stand-out athletic moments and long, memorable afternoons, it is also marred by twenty-three years of a shameful exclusivity. Though no signs proclaimed it, Tempe's Mexican-American community was barred from the site until May 21, 1946, when returning Mexican-American veterans won their fight to integrate the pool.

In Tempe, as in many southern states at the time, such segregation was "an almost uniform practice," upheld by "state regulation of a non statutory nature, by local ordinance, and by prevailing custom." Light-skinned Mexican-Americans could pass for white—as could light-skinned African-Americans in the South—and gain admission to the pool, but if "they were seen with their darker skin friends they would not be admitted again, because then it was known that they too were Mexican/Mexican American." An exception was made for the family of Antonio Celaya, a long-established merchant in town, and light-skinned as well.

Such discrimination is particularly upsetting given the long history of friendly relationships between Anglos and Mexicans in old-time Tempe. As far back as 1871 many Mexican employees of the Tempe Irrigating Canal Company became shareholders; several even rose to direct the company, while many Anglo men married Mexican women. At that time those of Mexican descent represented eighty-five percent of the town's 900 citizens. Racism became common, however, around 1900 when the Mexicans became a minority. A factor in this changing attitude was the Mexican Revolution of 1910 during which many Mexicans crossed the border to escape the current hardships at home. That many of these immigrants were low-skilled workers would henceforth tarnish the image of Mexicans—even those who had been in the country for many years. To distinguish themselves from these recent immigrants, long-time Tempeans might assert a Spanish heritage to escape discrimination: "Anglos understood Spaniards to be white and native to the region, while denigrating Mexicans as non-white immigrants."

Two case studies in discrimination at Tempe Beach paint a picture of these trying times, those of Lillie Perez in 1936 and of two Mexican-American women and their Mexican dates in 1942. The 1936 event stemmed from a happily anticipated field trip to the pool by students from St. Mary's School in Phoenix on May 21st. These students, a group known as the "Children of Mary," were being admitted to the pool when Lillie Perez, accompanied by her mother—a chaperone for the trip— was denied admittance on the basis of her nationality. A letter of protest, signed by the chaperones as well as a priest, describes in legalese what happened next: "...although said lady or priest endeavored to persuade the manager to admit said child to the swimming pool, explaining that she was a decent and respectable child belonging to a respectable family and that she had never before been refused admittance anywhere on account of her nationality, nevertheless she was refused admittance by the manager."

In a last-ditch effort to persuade this manager, the chaperones informed him that two other Spanish or Mexican children from the club were already admitted and swimming in the pool. Instead of relenting, or at least 'letting it go this time,' "said manager did then and there approach Adeline and Pauline Loza, and made them leave said pool on account of their nationality, thereby greatly humiliating and embarrassing them before the other children." Not surprisingly no redress was achieved by this letter of protest.

Six years later, in early June, 1942, two Mexican-American women and their Mexican dates (pilots in training at Williams Air Force base) were similarly barred from Tempe Beach. In a striking display of insensitivity, not only to this foursome, but to the spirit of the times, the pool thus turned away two men who were "in the United States as America's allies in a war against fascism, and who were honoring the intent of the principles behind President Roosevelt's 'Good Neighbor Policy.'" In fact, just two months earlier, on April 18th, Mrs. John R. Murdock, wife of an Arizona congressman, had given an address on Pan

Americanism at ASU in observance of Pan-American Day.

Yet Maria Garcia, a member of the League of United Latin American Citizens Council 110, who made this case to Tempe's leaders, had no more success than did those who wrote the St. Mary's letter. Mayor W. W. Cole reacted to her complaint by denying his power to control a pool that had been leased to the Tempe Chamber of Commerce. Max Connolly, president of the Chamber, then claimed himself powerless to effect change without approval from both the chamber's board and the Tempe Beach Committee, headed by Dr. Reginald Stroud, who harbored a well-known disdain for both Mexicans and Mexican-Americans.

Garcia's objections did, however, spark a feeble attempt at remedy. That August the Tempe Beach Committee put forth $500 to build a second swimming pool exclusively for those of Mexican heritage. In 1939 an identical amount had been pledged by the Committee for this separate, but not so equal, pool to be built between the two buttes just north of the Hayden Canal. Construction of this 40x75 foot pool with a depth of two to eight feet was projected to cost a thousand dollars. Nothing materialized from this initial pledge, however, and by 1942 wartime rationing had made the scheme unachievable.

There would be one more attempt to garner funds for this separate pool, in 1944, but the project was ultimately scrapped. It was a poor solution to the problem anyway—hardly an answer to the obvious injustice of excluding a group of tax-paying citizens whose monies helped pay for the upkeep of the city pool on the basis of their heritage. In the end, Tempe Beach maintained its restrictions, and for four more years Tempe's Mexican-American citizens were barred from the swimming pool in their home town.

To read about these two shameful incidents at Tempe Beach is to realize how many such indignities must have been suffered—daily reminders of one's own deemed rank in a bifurcated town that advantaged Anglos. The Tempe History Museum has taped these stories and transcribed many. In one Josie Ortega Sanchez describes a near carbon copy of the St. Mary's field trip. The only difference is a greater awareness by this Tempe school in planning their ditch day in the forties:

"We voted that we wanted to go to Tempe Beach and have a picnic and go swimming. Well, that was fine and dandy, until the day before when the teacher gathered all the Mexican kids and told us that we could join the picnic but we couldn't go swimming, we weren't allowed to go swimming at the old Tempe Swimming Pool. He also told one of the girls—Rita Bustamante—because she was VERY, very light-complected and her hair was kind of blondish, reddish-blonde—he told her that SHE could go swimming if she wanted to, but the rest of us, because we were dark-skinned, we couldn't. So the mother of one of the girls found out about that—Dora Gonzales' mother, Maria Gonzales—opened her home up to us...so we all gathered over there—except for Rita Bustamante, she went swimming, and to this day I resent that."

In another interview, Elizabeth Montanez Rivera remembers riding on a garbage truck with her older brother up and down the streets by Tempe Beach while calling out, "Let us go swimming; let us go swimming; there is nothing wrong with the Mexican children." Still other tapes tell of clandestine swims under cover of darkness or of sanctioned ones on that special day that was ear marked for Mexicans, the day at the end of which the pool would be cleaned. As Dan Arredondo recalls: "It was either Monday or Thursday; I think it was Thursday because that's when they drained the pool. The water was all murky. But, hey, the grease won't come off these Mexicans. It'll be fine!" The day of that interview we laughed at this absurdity, but back then, when Dan was a child, the message was a noxious one, that Mexicans, being dark skinned, were therefore dirty—so dirty, in fact, that any water, once they had swum in it, would have to be drained.

This practice was not exclusive to Tempe Beach. A more extreme version took place in Miami, some eighty miles to the east of Tempe. There, instead of two swimming pools, the town supported two YMCAs, one for Anglos and one, just a building away, for Mexicans. The Mexican Y had an old piano and a pool table; the Anglo Y had weight-lifting, boxing, and swimming in a pool that was slowly drained over two days every week, Friday and Saturday. The Mexican children were invited to swim on Saturday mornings at the end of this process. As Ray Flores describes it: "As we were swimming around, the water was going down, and after awhile we were like tadpoles swimming around at the bottom of the pool just playing at swimming." Beyond merely insulting this segment of the population, Miami came close to making literal a common German catchphrase—to throwing the baby out with the bath water.

Given the belittlement of Mexican-Americans in more than one Arizona town, the grace of some victims is truly impressive as they speak, without rancor, of these difficult times. Alex Calderon, for example, has this to say about those after-hours swims: "We used to sneak into the swimming pool at night to swim....at that age we did not know the word 'prejudice' and we held no malice in our hearts for those who were prejudiced." Just as magnanimous is Alex Arredondo in reflecting on a place that excluded him when he was young: "Tempe's a fine place, a fine place. It's growing. It had the same growing pains as everybody else had at the time."

Nevertheless, if Tempe could be likened to a child in the throes of growing pains, that child was a decidedly slow learner. In fact, that child could be accused of deliberately failing to see the light, of willfully protracting its moral education. In 1943, for example, when a federal judge ruled unconstitutional the segregation of a California pool, the town's response was not to see itself in that ruling but instead to assert that the case did not apply to them. Their rationale involved leases. In 1931 Tempe Beach was leased for five years to the Chamber of Commerce. A year later the lease was renegotiated for ten years, set to expire in 1942. In 1944—after the federal ruling against the pool—the lease was again renegotiated for a ten-year period and dated retroactively to 1942. Clearly, this manipulation of the leasing contracts was a method of circumventing the new law. As Christine Marin explains in her article on the battle for civil rights in Tempe and Phoenix during the forties:

"The Tempe Beach committee believed that the federal ruling had no bearing over swimming pool regulations enforced by a citizens' committee. After all, they reasoned, no city laws nor ordinances had been violated or broken. While the discrimination against Mexicans and Mexican Americans was unconstitutional in spirit and wrong morally, it was apparently not unlawful because there were no written city laws nor city codes declaring Tempe Beach to be segregated and not open to Mexicans and Mexican Americans."

Ray Martinez, head of American Legion Thunderbird Post 41 in Phoenix, concurs with this assessment: "Tempe Beach had some federal assistance in developing the park, so if the city controlled it the park couldn't discriminate because there were federal funds involved. But what they did then was they leased Tempe Beach to the Junior Chamber of Commerce. The Junior Chamber of Commerce then tacked on the discrimination clause." Clearly, as long as the pool was leased to the Chamber and regulated by the Tempe Beach Committee, segregation would continue at Tempe Beach.

For those of us gripped by nostalgia for our childhood pool, looking back at its dishonorable past is a painful process. My happy memories of the sounds of Tempe Beach—the jukebox, the creaking gate, the cannonballs, the lifeguards' whistles—appear less enchanting when imagined from just blocks away, circa

1940, when a Mexican-American child would have been listening as she sweltered in the desert heat. Projecting my birth back some fifteen years, I can imagine myself, so often mistaken for Mexican, being stopped at the bathhouse door and maybe even turned away. When not envisioning myself as a victim, I can see my own complicity in the impulse that closed off the swimming pool to a segment of its citizens: The discrimination at Tempe Beach was a darker version of The Pink Shadow Club—founded, as it was, on that same tribal drive.

An antidote to this grim remembering is to pan eastward from the swimming pool, past Mill, past College, past Rural, past McClintock to where the Arredondo boys were growing up, out of earshot of Tempe Beach and maybe not missing everything at all, given the canal with its sandy bottom and the cottonwoods shading them as they swam: "The canal ran parallel to 8th Street, right by the Creamery, right by those apartments, comes into ASU, where fraternity row is—it's now underground; you just don't see it—comes out up toward the butte. It used to go through the mill, the old Tempe canal, and ended up in the Alameda ditch (Alex)." Dan remembers learning to swim there as a child: "It was clean, pretty nice. And there was a Japanese family that lived down on the canal there. We'd go down there and swim in the water. We had great fun—big cottonwood trees over the top. We'd go down there when we were young kids, and that's when people couldn't swim over here [at Tempe Beach]."

Swimming in the Canal

Left to their own devices, these children had corrected the town's deviation from a civic ideal, had created a space that would presage an integrated swimming pool, the one that two decades later Tom and Bobby Valdez would set out for, running two miles, maybe two-and-a-half, full speed in the summer sun, "clean to Tempe Beach."

Other Voices

The High Diving Board
"That was way up there for us kids."

The high diving board at Tempe Beach was to the pool what the Hayden Flour Mill was to the town, a looming focal point around which the pool's activity revolved. If not on the diving board or queued up on the ladder, one was watching from the pool below. And so the board became not only a platform for launching dives but a kind of stage with a ready-made audience—the swimmers and sunbathers down below. On the board, the diver knew that the audience was on her side, that there would be no jeers or mockery however badly her attempt might end. The climate created by the life-guard crew thus extended to the diving board: the leniency they practiced in the waters below carried over to this hazardous space, insuring that whatever wounds might be suffered there, one's ego would remain intact. Ray Oldenburg might be speaking of Tempe Beach in describing the ease of this true Third Place: "Here individuals may uncork that which other situations require them to bottle up....Here the stage is available, and it's a wonderful stage, for the audience appreciates the actor no matter how bad the act."

As many actors as divers climbed up the ladder to the three-meter board, many of them testing out stand-up routines. A common one was The Frightened Child. This involved a melodramatic acting out of abject terror—hand-wringing, halting steps toward the end of the board, a look at the water below, a terrified retreat, another slow advance, a shocked reaction, a swifter retreat—until the patience of those on the ladder wore thin and the lifeguard would blow his whistle, at which point The Frightened Child would morph into The Seasoned Pro and leap off the board, maybe yelling out "Geronimo." Jeff remembers a variation on this routine where the actor began as The Seasoned Pro:

"Emmett Aepli and I used to pull a dumb trick. When Emmett did it I would laugh uncontrollably. It consisted of doing the standard wait for your turn on the high dive, but once up there taking an inordinate amount of time "figuring out" your complicated, daring dive. It meant holding your head in concentration, checking the tension of the board, doing little hand gestures imitating the number of flips and such. When everyone was angry with impatience, and others not in line were awaiting the incredible dive, Emmett would finally run off the board like some sort of spastic dork and crash unceremoniously into the pool. Why that was so funny to me I still don't understand."

Jeff and Emmett had clearly intuited the concept of bathos, the "ludicrous descent from the exalted or lofty to the commonplace." Such anticlimax produces laughter every time.

Steve remembers his derivative performances based on "The Three Stooges" TV show: "I used to enjoy doing a Curly Joe imitation on the diving board. 'Woo-Woo-Woo-Woo.' And the Curly Joe step then was perhaps a precursor to Michael Jackson's Moonwalk, a backward kick. You'd go back and then forward, and then you'd jump and try to land without getting hurt but still be funny about it." He remembers another TV-based stunt, inspired by those early Westerns ("Roy Rogers," "Wild Bill Hickok," "The Cisco Kid") where, pretending to be shot and staggering to the end of the board, he would then fall off, clutching the bullet wound in his chest.

Though my brothers were not the only clowns to perform on the high dive at Tempe Beach, they may have the longest memories. Jeff recalls a time he did a canine sketch the whole length of the diving board: "I remember once starting on "all fours" and firing full steam to the edge, then toppling over in a frenzy. The knees suffered a few raspberries from the coarse edges of the board." Jeff also offers an explanation for the prevalence of comedy on that high, exposed space: "I think making a joke of it was our way, psychologically speaking, to mask what was, after all, a real fear. That was way up there for us kids."

For me, the fear reached its climax on those last two rungs of the ladder, then dissipated as I took the board. For others on occasion those last rungs inspired a change of heart, at which point those of us on the ladder would move aside as the child would make his way back down. I don't remember anyone laughing at this unceremonious backing out. We could all relate. The only hint of unkindness I recall was the sudden spotlight turned on a diver by the shout-out of his "friend" below: "ALL EYES ON THE HIGH BOARD!" On hearing this we could no more avert our eyes than not think of an elephant when advised against doing so. Still, like everything else at Tempe Beach, this antic was accepted as all in good fun.

Not everyone, however, was looking for laughs as they climbed up the ladder of the three-meter board. Some were looking for girls. For the teenage boy, the high-board became the equivalent of a hot rod idling at the light. By peeling out, the driver could turn the heads of the girls in the neighboring car, just as here, by executing the cannonball, he could lay the equivalent of rubber on the road. The messy splash of the cannonball resulted from the boy's compacting of his body mid-way through the jump as his arms encircled his upraised knees. He entered the water in an ugly squat, creating a sound that was as much the point as the towering spray. The bigger the boy, the louder the boom when the human ball made contact with the pool. His bulk was also a factor in the preface to this crashing sound: the rattle of the board as he sprang into the air. These sounds, in their amplitude, established the diver's potency and therefore his rank in the hierarchy that was Tempe Beach. Next to the lifeguards, the master of the splash dive was most convincing in his courtship display. Without the advantage of red trunks and whistle, he made the most of that watery blast.

Though no girl attempted the cannonball, put off, perhaps, by its gracelessness, the figure four appealed to all. It could be, in fact, a beautiful sight, begun with a high spring, then a smooth descent, arms raised overhead, until at the eleventh hour the diver would lean back and slice into the water, holding one knee bent against the chest. When perfectly performed, the entry would create a delayed reaction as the water seemed to suck into a vortex, then spew back out. When it was done right, the diver could feel her success in the pocket created around her body and hear the sound that ensured a spray. Still, underwater she could never be sure. Many of us learned the art of the white lie while watching our friends do figure fours at Tempe Beach. "Did I splash?" they would ask upon surfacing. And we would always assure them, "Yes, you did." Creating a splash, however, did not necessarily signal success. As Tom Voss recalls: "The figure four was my favorite dive, except for the time the water hit my face and gave me a bloody nose." From that height, anything could go painfully wrong.

Waiting on the ladder with the comics and the splashers were the people who actually intended to dive. These were the ones who, seeking thrills, would risk life and limb to add to their repertoire—to turn another somersault, or upgrade a tuck dive into a pike. From this ten-foot height the simplest maneuver was anything but. Everyone who dived there has a tale of woe. For Steve, the problem was the head-first entry:

"On occasion I would have the nerve to dive in head-first from the high board. If you went in with your hands spread apart the water would smack you so hard you'd think twice about doing that again. Then I learned to cup my hands in a little arrow that would cleave the water and keep my head from getting smacked. Thirty-five years later I tried a similar dive off the high board at the local Chandler pool not realizing I had aged somewhat. I hit the water wrong, flipped over backwards, tore my rotator cuffs and other various tendons off the bone and had to have surgery."

For David Link, the problem was not the dive but the flip: "I remember trying to do a flip off the high dive and the sound of a sharp crack as I hit the water flat on my back. I think the stinging stopped somewhere around October." Daf accepted her siblings' challenge to do a double from the three-meter board, and ended in a similar fix: "I opened up too late and landed flat on my face, knocking the wind out of me. When I came to the surface, the lifeguard was in the water." For girls, the aftermath of the misdive could be characterized by more than pain: Diane (Follette) Lisonbee remembers a swimsuit malfunction: "For me, total Belly Flop AND my swimsuit top was around my neck as I struggled to the surface."

For some of us, the problem was not the water but the board. Keith Sipes remembers an encounter with it at a formal meet: "At the State finals meet in Phoenix I hit the board on the one-meter round and continued on with the three-meter bleeding from the nose and face. I finished seventh or eighth in the state and the top three from that meet actually won Olympic medals. Quite a strong field. I still have my ribbon." Charlene (Mills) Ashworth hit the board while performing an inward dive one evening when it was just getting dark: "My mouth caught the board, and it felt like I had knocked several teeth out." In the end she had lost just one tooth, but even with the lifeguards' help never managed to find it." I have no memory of a freak collision with the one-meter board that Daf still recalls: "We were learning the gainer, and you went up, did your somersault, and landed on your feet right back on the board." When I asked her what happened next, she said, "You did it again and landed in the water."

It is hard to imagine how I could forget such a shocking impact, or how it could have come about. But even divers more experienced than I would sometimes misjudge their distance from the board. In fact, it would be that same group, the gainers or "reverse dives," that would almost do in Greg Louganis in the 1988 Summer Games. Still a fan of diving twenty-five years later, I was watching the Olympics on TV when he hit his head while doing a reverse dive from the three meter board (a two-and-a-half pike) and then, after pausing for stitches, climbed right back up to nail the next dives, thus qualifying for the final round and, eventually, winning gold. I remember marveling at his courage that day. What none of us knew then was that he was battling a greater fear than the diving board. Having hidden from the world that he was then infected with HIV, he must have been conflicted about whether he should tell or not, having just bled into the diving tank, then had a doctor stitch him up. In 1988 few of us knew how fragile the AIDS virus really is. Louganis must have agonized, and not from his head wound.

Whatever one attempted, there was sure to be drama on the three-meter board. There was also growth. On the high board we learned to overcome our fears while never forgetting how those fears felt. We all can recall a moment like the one described by JoAnn (Voss) Brown: "My brother double-dog dared me to dive off that thing. You should have seen the line of kids waiting for me while I stood up there scared ****less. But I did it." No self-esteem movement was needed for those of us who tackled that diving board nor schooling in compassion. It all happened there in that lengthening line, and on that precipice, steeling our nerves before taking the plunge.

The Snack Bar
"The meat was marbled in different colors we'd never
seen in hamburgers."

If the high dive at Tempe Beach was an airy
platform over the pool, the snack bar was its deep
under-belly, a kind of boiler-in-the-hold that pumped
out food and music and popsicle sticks for our plunging
games. From the moment the bath house opened its
doors, the jukebox played, its melodies providing the
tracks that would score our lives well beyond the
closing of the swimming pool.

That music was a marketing ploy, a siren's lure to
the children with coins in the pockets of their cut-off
jeans. Dan Arredondo learned the trick from the
manager who came before: "He told me 'Here's what
you have to do. As soon as you get in there and the pool
opens up, always put some money in the machine.' And
the song we had in there was 'Itsy-Bitsy Teeny-Weeny.'
We'd put it on there, blast it out." After that initial play,
I'm not sure who fed the jukebox at the snack-bar stand;
I only know there was a never a lull. The coins kept
dropping as a top-ten set-list cycled through, then
through again, until a certain selection would wear a
groove in our cortex folds and, so established, be ever-
bound to our memories of Tempe Beach.

As would the smells and taste of food—hamburgers
and hot dogs, popcorn and soft-serve cones, but mostly
the candy that, more often than not, was all we children
could afford. A nickel could buy the most often-cited
purchase from the snack bar stand, with its various
names—"Neapolitan taffy," "Ice-cream taffy," "those

taffy sheets." Susan (Abbott) Holmboe remembers them being "about the thickness of three sheets of paper with a chocolate, vanilla and strawberry stripe. Left in the sun they were quite soft, but would easily crack if cold." Also mentioned were the Big Hunk, the Payday, and the Zero bar, Bit-o-Honey, and Bazooka Joe gum, each pink square dusted with sugar, then wrapped in a waxy full-color cartoon. The snack-bar worker would hand the candy through the window servicing the swimming pool or through the other, open to the people outside in the park. That second window figures in a scene still recalled by my brother Steve:

"I remember once going to the snack bar and buying my Bit-o-Honey when Johnny the Mexican appeared at the window on the other side. And Johnny looked over and said, 'I'll pay for his.' I told my parents about this, and they advised me to stay away from Johnny the Mexican because they thought that you shouldn't take candy from strangers. But he really wasn't like that."

I wonder if they also advised him to drop "the Mexican" from Johnny's name, demeaning as it was (though not meant to be) and also unneeded in referencing the figure that everyone knew, a fixture of our small-town's core: Johnny on his bicycle.

When not being treated to candy bars, Steve would buy himself gum. One day with his purchase he got more than he'd bargained for, a preteen mishap that still resonates today:

"My biggest bubble gum story, oh maybe back in '62, I blew a large bubble and a girlfriend of one of the lifeguards popped it; it collapsed into my face and got tangled up in my eyebrows, my eyelashes and my hair and I became the center of attention. They brought me to the bathhouse and I put my head in this girl's lap as they worked feverishly to remove the bubblegum. They had a sort of solvent—maybe it was Bactine—or acetone or something, trying to get this stuff out of my hair and eyes, and then they got out scissors to cut out pieces of it, and I was just lavished with attention and it was one of the greatest moments of my life [laughs]. I knew that I would be telling this story for weeks to come."

Other common snack-bar buys were the Push-up, the Drumstick, the Popsicle, and especially the Bullet, that frozen treat with its signature ridges so fondly remembered—except by Fred Stone, who regrets its purchase at an end-of-school party at Tempe Beach: "I remember Tempe Beach for two reasons, neither of them great memories. I fell from the top of the slide and hit the concrete below, and I spent a treasured 1908 dime when it got mixed up in other loose change when buying a Bullet at the refreshment stand." Fred can take comfort in the fact that that long-lost dime, mingling as it had been with other coins in his pocket that day, would be rated somewhat less than "fine" and would thus bring only a few dollars today. On the other hand, who can measure the value of a Bullet bar, consumed on the lawn by the snack bar stand after swimming in the waters of Tempe Beach on the very cusp of summertime? Even purchased with a decades-old dime, that popsicle would have been a steal.

I don't remember ever eating real food at the snack bar stand— hamburgers, hot dogs, or the bean tostados that Cindy (Statz) Mattoon remembers being "the BEST." That griddle smell I do recall wafting over the deep end and rising to the high dive where it tormented those of us whose parents had neglected to fund our lunch. Deborah "Campbell" Austin was one of these: "I don't remember ever eating anything. I guess Mom didn't give us any money." We five Cole kids suffered too. Tom has a vivid memory of watching Billy Richardson put hot sauce on a hamburger, while he sat (empty-bellied) by.

Tom can take comfort today in the revelation from Alan Holly, a snack-bar worker, that the hungry child at Tempe Beach might have been better off than the sated one. Though he and fellow worker Richard Rickel could eat anything for free, they soon learned to steer clear of griddle fare:

"The meat was marbled in different colors we'd never seen in hamburgers—yellows and greens—so we actually brought food from home and cooked it up or put it in the refrigerator and ate it, but we didn't eat the food there. We did drink the soda and we did eat the popcorn and, oh, they had ice cream, soft-serve, and that was about it. And the fries were—I don't know what was wrong with the fries, but we never ate the fries either."

That food must have been truly bad if Alan—fifteen years old, beginning his shift straight from swim practice, and licensed to eat anything for free—willingly abstained. Richard, on the other hand, made the most of his employee perk while still avoiding the mystery meat. According to Alan: "Richard claims that, because of all the soda-drinking, that year cost his parents a fortune well beyond what we made because of his teeth getting ruined from all the sugar."

Despite these drawbacks, a job at the snack-bar must have been a plum, placing one in the very center of the social scene, near the pulsating music that drew in teens and the baseball field that attracted a wealth of female fans. The power to distribute food conferred on the snack-bar worker a certain status that could easily have been abused by giving away food to his latest crush. Why this didn't happen, Alan explained:

"It was my first job, other than mowing lawns and things like that, and I went in and interviewed with him [the concessionaire], and somewhere in the middle of the interview he felt the need to address issues like giving away food. And he made a big impression on me. To this day I remember he said, 'If I catch you giving any food out you will lose your manhood,' but he used different words and different expressions as to how that was going to occur....So I didn't give any food away."

Dan Arredondo, an earlier concessionaire, ensured his profits through less brutal means, by keeping the money close to home: "It was just me, and then my family would help." Millie Loughrige remembers picking up Dan's mother on her way to the pool when Dan was called in to the Army Reserves, and the family took over while he was gone. By the end of the summer Dan had pulled in more than a lifeguard or even a manager. It is easy to see why:

"You're an independent contractor, and there were only two things you had to buy: the soda machine and the jukebox. The freezer belonged to the city; the grill was built-in....They had windows to the outside so you could service the park, and there used to be a skating rink right on the outside there, and then on the inside of course you had all the people coming from the pool. We had a captive audience."

Not to mention a famished one, too hungry after hours of swimming to notice that the burgers were mottled and the fries sub-par or to care if they were. At the snack-bar every day was the dining equivalent of fifth-day water. We ate in the same way that we swam. As Alex Arredondo noted, while adults would arrive on the first days after the pool had been drained, "You kids would swim no matter what." And eat whatever.

I remember the snack bar as the place where the child encountered the teen; where the careless tossed their cigarette butts, and the caring shared their taffy sheets; where the world passed by: lifeguards, bathhouse workers, children from various Tempe schools, parents and coaches and Johnny at the outside window, buying a young boy's candy bar. It is no surprise that such a place would spawn a legend, like that of Schwab's Pharmacy where Lana Turner's mere presence on a bar stool would make her a star. That parallel moment occurred one day in the early sixties when Alex saw Don Wilkinson working in the snack bar and asked John Hollis about making him a guard:

"Don was an athlete at Tempe High, and I said I thought he'd make a great lifeguard. So we pulled him out of the snack bar and I gave him a real quick Senior Lifesaving course and trained him a little bit so he could get his badge....Don became a great lifeguard and went on to become the Aquatic Director of the City of

Tempe, so he directed all three pools for awhile: McClintock, Tempe Beach, and Clark Park."

Though the snack bar at Tempe Beach produced mediocre food, it set one man on the path to success. Today, though defunct for fifty years, it still serves up memories (USDA Prime) of the place where people gathered as the popcorn popped and the jukebox played, smells and sounds intermingling like the coins in our pockets: Buffalo nickels, a 1908 dime.

Third-Day Water

Memoir

At Tempe Beach the summer I turned thirteen, puberty brought with it only half of the fate I had foreseen the summer before, shaking my hair onto those frozen statues who were Wendy and Mary Jane posed on their towels by the lifeguard stand. Daf and I were as active as ever as we rolled out the door every morning, our fat-tired bikes pointing north toward the riverbed and diving practice at Tempe Beach. We took our first plunge at eight a.m. and kept it up until the pool threw open its gates at ten. We were hard and lean—impossibly tanned—our shoulders broadening, our sinews stretching as we tucked and arched and piked our way through those long summer days. Years later, when I am forty-five, a student who's forgotten my name will describe me to a colleague in terms that will call up my diving years: "She's small and dark with broad shoulders." "I knew immediately who he meant," my colleague will say.

I can still see Daf on that old blue bike I followed behind, the shape of her legs, as we pedaled down the sidewalk on Mill (before the advent of bike lanes) past the Dairy Queen, the Casa Loma and the Boston Store, Joe Sellah's Sporting Goods and the Casa Vieja to the waiting waters of Tempe Beach. We might pass Johnny on his beat-up bike or a dog on its morning stroll (before the advent of leash laws). It never crossed our minds that a younger Johnny would have swum in canals, but not at the Beach, so ignorant were we of the history behind the very pool we were headed toward. We were clueless as well as shoeless, dressed only in our one-piece suits, and carrying only towels—no coverups, no combs or lotions (before the advent of sunscreen). We were motion itself, from the spinning tires of our bicycles to the high rotations of our spring-board dives.

Puberty had hardly slowed us down, but had altered our allegiances, had stifled us in subtle ways so that behind our motion was a new compliance, a hard-core focus on getting it right. We were willing apprentices, shaping our motion to the templates of another's devising: we counted off the steps of our approaches as instructed, raised and lowered our arms on cue, pointed our toes, and hoped for approval in the form of scores from a panel of judges who would bless or condemn us at organized meets in neighboring pools.

Daf and I, core members of the Tempe Beach Diving Team, learned our craft from the lifeguard Chuck, who would meet us at the pool at eight and put us through our paces. His method could be characterized as trial and error, our follow-through as hit or miss. We would spring from the board into that ten-foot chasm, our bodies contorted into new positions, charting novel flight paths to the water below. Before each dive we would muster our courage, review Chuck's instructions ("Try it"), and synchronize our lift-off to the ebb and flow of the swim team practice being held below. The lifeguard Marvin, muscle-bound, would blow his whistle, the swimmers would push off, a few seconds later Daf or I would lift off the diving board, the water would part to accept our bodies, we would surface (in pain or glory); then the fastest swimmers would return, and Daf or I would reclimb the ladder, recalculate, and dive again. There was no time to hesitate, to regroup from failure; what must have looked like courage was merely a function of the limited real estate under the board.

Still, I remember being afraid. One morning Chuck decided to fill in a gap in my repertoire. I had only one of the two required dives from the back position off the three-meter board. "Let's try," he improvised, "the back one and half... pike position. It'll be great." I was less sure. The back position was my downfall. I had no fear of the inward dive, standing backward and then turning in toward the diving board, nor even the reverse dive, starting off forward and then arching backwards in the air, the board passing close to one's open face. But to stand facing backwards on a board that moved with every toe flex, high above the water, and blind to the space one was poised to enter, made me sick with fear. Now, Chuck had a plan. "Throw yourself back into your somersault," he told me, "and listen for my whistle. When you hear it, open up and reach for the water." Somehow I mustered the courage to flip myself back into a passable pike; I heard the whistle; I opened up— I landed flat on my back. The sound of my body hitting the water was as shocking as the pain. When I surfaced I heard Chuck saying, "Sorry, sorry, I blew the whistle too soon." And then the inevitable—"Try it again."

It's hard to imagine that soon I would do that dive in formal meets. Even harder to conceive is how I had moved—in two short years—from the creativity of Sally's Special through the satire of splay-toed water ballet to this outsourced back dive, a perfect metaphor *for what I'd become: a fully socialized female teen, entrusting her fate to the care of a male, a girl who by her fourteenth year had already lost her edge.*

Sometimes, instead of coaching, Chuck would take the board himself. His signature dive, as I recall, was a forward one-and-a-half with a full twist in open position, a dive I was never to master or even attempt. One morning Chuck convinced me to bring our family's movie camera to practice and we'd film our diving. Today, the film is too dark to make out, but I watched it enough to replay some sequences inside my head. I can still see Chuck, in perfect form, twisting and turning in the air above the high board; my body arching backward toward the low board in a good-enough reverse dive; an unfortunate entry occasioned by my arms spread wide apart instead of meeting above my head; a smiling Cindy Statz, treading water in the deep end, then swimming away in a crawl second only in beauty to the stroke of my mother; Marvin, redheaded, his eyes ever shaded; the high diving board looming always in the background—a Tempe Beach icon—with the open grill work of its ladder; the lane lines black beneath the water, that summer shimmer in the air. But now I'm uncertain whether I'm remembering or inventing, the dark film unable to verify what I recall.

Daf does have the medal to corroborate our diving coup for the team that year: a one-two finish on the one-meter board at the AAU Open Championships. The reality was somewhat different. When Daf and I competed in meets, we faced young divers trained at the famous Dick Smith Swim Gym in Phoenix. They had begun on trampolines, then moved on to diving boards with spotting belts—had never been subjected to pain nor had to watch for an open space before launching their dives. In fact, two years from the meet where Daf won that medal, Dick Smith would become the Women's Olympic Diving Coach. His girls could eat our lunch. Still, that morning, at breakfast tables all around the town, people read of our victory, of Sally Cole and Daphne Livingston winning gold and silver in this crucial meet. They would never know the secret to our win: Dick Smith's divers had been out of town at a more prestigious meet that day. Daf and I had been the only entrants.

Some twelve years from this day, when I will have ceased to think about Dick Smith and his formidable team, I will read of him in the newspaper. He will be one of only four survivors of a plane crash in American Samoa. While the other passengers had headed forward to escape, thus dying in the smoke and fire, Smith had survived by diving out an exit on the side, then leaping from the wing of the plane. I remember marveling, as I read, at the way this coach's expertise had come back round to rescue him, this man who had begun his career at the very pool where I'd learned to dive. In 1935 a young Dick Smith had won the Junior Low Board and Senior High Board titles at Tempe Beach, then "raced away on my bike and hid under the Tempe bridge," knowing his mother would learn of his prize. Only two years earlier Smith had been temporarily paralyzed when he hit the bottom after diving from the tower at the Riverside Pool and had promised his mother he would never dive again. Now photographers had blown his cover, sending him into hiding in the riverbed by Tempe Beach, where he would stay until "Finally my brother George found me down there and said come on home, Mom knows and she says it's OK."

Our mothers were fearful as well. Mine made me promise I would never go higher than the three- meter board, an easy vow to keep since there was no tower at Tempe Beach. Daf's forbade her to go along when we swam at the lakes in our high school years. Neither of them attended our meets. We were an unwatched generation, so different from our own children who never so much as practiced a sport without a parent in the stands. Back then the standard parenting style could be characterized as Benign Neglect. Our coach, Chuck, not our parents, would pick us up before the meets,

90

watch us during them, then return us when the meet was done.

I remember only once my mother showing up to watch. The pool, which one I don't recall, had a separate diving tank with chairs for spectators all around. During warmups for the three-meter contest, I was so nonplussed by the specter of my mother that in doing my standard practice dive, the forward one-and-a-half, I made an extra effort to impress her with my height, raising my head before bending into my somersault. As a result I didn't make it all the way around, landing in a near belly-flop right before her eyes. I remember Chuck saying, "What was that?" and feebly explaining. "It looked like it was going to be a really nice forward somersault," he added, and left it at that. A man barely out of his teens, he had somehow known how to highlight the positive in my disgrace: that nanosecond when, in the air, I had seemed to be in control of my dive.

My mother must have come again, though, bringing my father. I have a hazy memory of the three of us, after the meet, talking to the victor's coach (Dick Smith, of course) and their asking him if he would train me. Even when he said yes I knew it was not to be. My parents would never have paid for a coach. They camped, bird-watched, drove down to Rocky Point on weekends after work, played bridge, threw wild parties—but never once did I ever see them attend a professional sporting event or even watch a game on TV. Once for a short spell I remember my father playing catch with us in the backyard, but even then I had the feeling my mother had put him up to it. He had zero interest in sports, nor had my sister, Wendy, or my twin brothers Steve and Tom. The youngest, Jeff, and I must have been stolen from our cradles to be raised in this alien brood. Jeff ran marathons, entered five- and ten- K races across the country, and like me followed sports in the paper and on TV. My own three children would be trained by professional soccer coaches who would give me a glimpse into what that Swim Gym must have been like. "This match will be easy," they'd tell my children. "It's a Rec team." In other words a team from a playground, being coached by a volunteer. A part of me would always have a stake in the Rec team's performance. Daf and I, high on heart and low on skill, had been Rec to the core.

After practice on those summer mornings, the pool phone would often ring, with a friend's voice asking: "What day water is it?" Our response would be the critical factor in whether the caller would join us or not. "Third day," would almost always elicit a positive response, for as in the work week, the third day was when the shock of the week's beginning had just worn off and the slide into Friday had not yet begun. Third-day water, like Wednesday, was the point at which one settled in, temperature and chlorine briefly in sync until just one day later—the tipping point reached—we would paddle with bloodshot eyes through a cloudy mixture of debris (band-aids, old dibble dabble sticks) and just one day beyond that, the infamous fifth day, we'd be corned like beef in a gaseous brine.

Sometimes as Daf and I rode our bikes back home, she always in the lead, we'd stop at the Dairy Queen and buy a milkshake for 50 cents. We were shaky with *hunger, sunburned, exhausted from our active day. We'd ride on—one hand on the handlebars, the other gripping our dairy drink—past the Sellah's, down College, and around the park to Daf's house where I'd say good-bye, then continue across Broadway to mine. I'd clean my plate at dinner, head out, perhaps, for a softball game at Daley Park, then fall into bed, only to roll out in the morning, armed only with my towel, and follow Daf down Mill for another day at Tempe Beach.*

History

1943-1953
The Third Decade of Tempe Beach

Tempe Beach, circa 1943

When the summer season opened in 1943, Tempe Beach was still an Anglos-only pool. In late November, 1944, the Reverend Bernard Gordon of Tempe Catholic Church would hold a rally to build that long-imagined second pool for "the Mexican people of Tempe," but it was not until the end of World War II that the unifying culture of the battlefield would assert itself against the unfair practices at the city pool. Two organizations were instrumental in this fight. The first was Phoenix's LULAC 110, presided over by Placida Garcia Smith. It was this council's Maria Garcia who had taken her battle with Mayor Cole and Max Connolly all the way to the national LULAC convention in 1942. Although she would ultimately lose this fight, she had become inspired by New Mexico's Senator Dennis Chavez, whom she had informed of the incident at Tempe Beach and whose speech at the conference indirectly referenced it: The membership had, he told them, "the backing of the entire nation in its will to promote friendly relations in Latin America" as well as to battle injustice at home.

Real progress began to be made, however, when the now emboldened LULAC Council was joined in their battle by American Legion Thunderbird Post 41, newly established in 1945. Key figures in this organization were Phoenix veterans Frank "Pippa" Fuentes, Pete Martinez, Carlos Ontiveros and Ray Martinez, who ultimately commanded the post. Although the Phoenix members were focused on poverty and segregated housing in their neighborhoods, they agreed to play a supporting role in resolving the issue at Tempe Beach, relinquishing the lead to Tempe veterans Danny Rodriguez, Raymond Terminal, and Genaro Martinez so as not to appear as outside agitators interfering in another town's cause.

Ray Martinez recalls the planning that went into this crucial first fight: "Danny and Raymond—we would meet every day at six o'clock and plan our strategy." The men decided to patronize the businesses of Chamber members, thereby getting to know these men. Yet on those initial calls, the owners were nowhere to be seen. Rather than becoming discouraged, the veterans used a strategy of tact and resolve: "Have patience; wait; be polite; if it takes two hours, take turns; stay there." Eventually, their patience began to pay off as Chamber members started coming around. Martinez lists these supporters as well as the detractors in early Tempe:

"Dwight "Red" Harkins"...he was for Hispanic use of the park the same as anybody else. There were some others—the Curry family, John and Eddie Curry—they were for allowing Hispanics. Carr Mortuary—the Carr brothers, Laurence and Eddie—they were for allowing Hispanics. And they were all members of the Chamber of Commerce. There was a Nevitt, who had a service station; he was violently against it. There was a doctor who was very prominent in the neighborhood, Dr. Stroud; he was very much against it. And there were several others, but these two were very actively outspoken."

My favorite story about Red Harkins may be apocryphal. Martinez admits that he only heard it second hand. But it's true to his character that Harkins would challenge the Tempe Beach Committee and its infamous leader, Dr. Stroud:

"The pool committee said 'If you allow these Mexicans in there, they're gonna tear the damn thing up! We won't be able to keep up with the damage!' And Dwight "Red" Harkins said, 'Well, how much damage do you think they'll make?' 'At least ten thousand dollars worth!' So I heard that Harkins wrote out a check for the ten thousand dollars and said, 'Look. Here's a check. I'm going to give it to you. If they tear up the place you can go ahead and cash my check and pay for the damage.'" The story then projects into the future with that check, still uncashed, turning up in the effects of the late Dr. Stroud.

Mid-May of 1946 finds Harkins addressing a luncheon meeting of the Tempe Beach Committee. A front-page story in the *Tempe Daily News* describes his presentation: the results of a citizen-survey he took on admission policies at Tempe Beach, solutions offered by recreation leaders in Phoenix and Mesa, and suggested changes to the current guidelines for entry to the pool. In the meantime the Tempe veterans were lobbying for membership to the Chamber themselves as well as calling for a vote on the integration of the pool. Both issues were decided on May 21st, a day that would not only add to the Chamber three Mexican-American members, but ultimately usher in an era of fairness at Tempe Beach.

The news account of that vote, however, shows a still-conflicted Chamber. In a four-and-a-half-hour session that night—which included presentations by Rodriguez, Stroud, and Harkins—the body took two crucial votes. The first, allowing universal access to the pool, resulted in a 15-15 tie. The second captured the headline: "Chamber of Commerce Favors "Limited" Beach Admission of Mexican-Americans." By 23-6 the Chamber had opted to "open the pool to all Americans on a limited basis, the qualifications to be decided by the Beach committee, possibly with the restriction of its use to Tempe residents only." Given the history of the Tempe Beach Committee, it is not hard to guess what the basis for those limits might be.

Imagine, then, the town's surprise on awakening to find just one day hence the following sentence on the paper's front page: "Effective this afternoon, admission to Tempe Beach pool is accorded to local Americans of Mexican descent." A skillful reader of the earlier story might have wondered why votes on one issue totalled 29 while 30 had created the initial tie. But without the whistle-blower J. O. Grimes, the college dean who was there that night, we might never know how a vote to restrict gave way to one that dispensed with restrictions. Nor would we understand how far some would go to maintain segregation at Tempe Beach. In his letter dated May 24th, Dean Grimes explains:

"It was announced by the President that Proposition Two (unrestricted admission of Mexicans) failed to pass. Some of us who were seated at the back of the room did not learn until the following day that Proposition #2 did pass, and therefore the vote on Proposition #3 [limited access] was illegal and of no effect." As it turned out, the President himself had cast a vote against Proposition #2 after seeing the tally (15 for, 14 against) in clear violation of Roberts Rules of Order and had thereby created a tie. Grimes reminds the committee that before the vote the Chamber had agreed "Proposition Three would be voted on only if Proposition Two failed to carry," citing this fact as further proof that the vote on Proposition Three was void.

Obviously angered at this tainted vote, as well as at the attitude of city leaders, Grimes offers up his own prescription for admission restrictions at Tempe Beach: "Cleanliness of skin rather than color of skin should be the accepted basic principle for entry into any pool." In this he echoes the sentiments of Barbara Crumpler,

President of the Beta Phi Chapter of Kappa Delta Pi at ASU. In a letter to the Tempe Beach Committee dated May 13, 1946, she urges that "admission to the Tempe Beach swimming pool be on the basis of cleanliness rather than on racial difference." Grimes takes the argument one step further in adding to his code "cleanliness of conduct," and finally that "all swimmers speak English to the best of their ability. (This includes all so-called one-hundred percent whites who speak cuss-English and otherwise defy the English language.)" In a fitting coda to this years-long battle over entry rules at Tempe Beach, a second check provided by Dwight "Red" Harkins would remain uncashed: the one he wrote for $2500 to begin a lawsuit should the vote that night not go their way.

It would be two years after this new entrance policy was put in place—in the summer of 1948—that Alex Arredondo would make his first trip, three miles on foot, with a visiting friend to Tempe Beach: "I remember going swimming there when I was about eight years old, and what I remember most about it was the lifeguard by the name of Cady who lived down the street, and I got in trouble within fifteen minutes of entering the pool. He sat me down for running, and I think I spent most of the time sitting down watching all the kids swim. That was my first memory."

It is hard to miss the irony of the now-sanctioned eight year old ending up in the same position he had been in before: watching from afar as the other kids swam. He could hardly have imagined that eleven years later he would be on the other side of that dynamic, blowing his whistle at the children running along the pool deck or swimming beneath the diving boards. Three years beyond that would find him managing the very pool that had been off-limits to him and his brothers not long before. In 1962 he would beat out eleven contenders to take over as the pool's aquatic director, just as a decade before his brother Dan had been the Beach's first lifeguard and manager of Mexican descent. With a characteristic generosity some fifty years later, Alex will remember how he got that job: "Vic Palmer, bless his heart, he said, 'Hey, I'm gonna open it up.' He didn't make a big show of it, and they were ready to take that chance. Everybody approved it when he said, 'I'm going to take my chances with this guy.'"

Tempe Daily News Headline 1962

Clearly, the vote in the Chamber of Commerce that night had affected the lives of one Tempe family. It would also affect the curriculum of Tempe High since a Phys-Ed swim class could now be held just a bus-ride away at Tempe Beach. It would also inspire reforms in other towns around the state. As the Reverend Manny Oliveras tells it: "This example of courage had a rippling effect, and in 1952 caused me to struggle to desegregate the pool in Granite Dells in Northern Prescott."

Back home, years later, that vote would linger as—unusual for a small town pool—the Beach would become a model of diversity. While pools in the South, as late as the seventies, were being drained and closed rather than integrate, in the early sixties (maybe earlier) buses were pulling up to Tempe Beach (perhaps from a Phoenix YMCA); moments later, the shallow end was a checkerboard of black and white. It is this that Cindy Whatley, then six, remembers—not the jukebox, or the snack bar or any high-dive mishap, but this: "Seeing black people in the pool and marveling at the color of their skin. I had seen Indians before, but never a black person. They seemed so foreign, so profoundly different."

Such was the legacy, the trickle-down, of the vote that night, that a new generation would encounter in their hometown pool what they otherwise would seldom see, and by intermingling become exposed to a world outside the confines of their town. The stubborn child that was Tempe Beach had recovered from its growing pains and had come of age, as in turn would we, in an integrated swimming pool.

Death at Tempe Beach
"...the drain held its victim."

Throughout our childhood, a story linking death and Tempe Beach passed from towel to towel along the lawn beside the swimming pool. It had all the markings of an urban legend in its quality of "mystery, horror, and fear" and in its function as a cautionary tale for those of us who, in our underwater plunges, had explored the drain at the pool's north-west end. In our tale, long ago a man had been sucked into that drain and drowned. Little did we know, the story was true.

It happened just eleven months before the vote to integrate the pool, at 6:30 pm on April 25th, 1945, when an airman from Luke Field made the fatal decision to do a good deed. Charles Thornberg, a twenty-year-old from Huntington, West Virginia, had hitchhiked to the pool that day as he often did to meet his friend, lifeguard Charlie Smith, then in the process of draining the pool. Having opened up the drain from the poolside with a long-handled wrench, Smith then realized he had begun the process too early in the evening. But when he tried to reclose the drain, a rod slipped out of its socket, and the wrench failed to function. Thornberg volunteered to reinsert the rod by hand and dived into the pool.

One can only imagine the force of the suction as six-hundred thousand gallons of water were funneling through a two-foot drain. Thornberg had swum too close to that drain and was hopelessly stuck. Smith and three others at the pool that day spent thirty minutes attempting to free him, but in the end it would take

Tempe and Williams Field fire trucks and two Civilian Defense pumps almost three hours to empty the pool and recover the body that was plugging up the drain. Even when the pool was emptied, the drain held its victim. As Marvin Williams (then a young teen) remembers, "They had to put ropes on and pull him out of there." Paul Aldridge, who would later lifeguard at the Beach, recalls that day too. Looking out the window from the family car as it crossed the bridge, he saw the huge crowd of people encircling the pool.

Thornberg's will be remembered as the only drowning at Tempe Beach. His sacrifice, however, will be forgotten. Almost two decades later, as his story passes from child to child, this "regular patron of the last two seasons," this helpful friend, will have been recast as a pool-hopping villain, who had climbed the fence to swim that night and thus deserved his own demise.

By that time a metal cage will have been constructed around the drain but still, as Dan Arredondo explains, "Even a grill would pin you up against it; there was a lot of suction." The only way to prevent another after-hours drowning at Tempe Beach was to institute a regular pre-draining drill:

"We would close the pool and walk around to make sure nobody was there; then we'd open the gate, and we couldn't start until maybe quarter after nine or so to start draining. By that time everybody was out. We'd walk around, make sure everybody was out, look down on the bottom because you know Thursday nights the pool was so dirty down there you couldn't see the bottom. We were very cautious about making sure the pool was empty."

Such prudence explains the brevity of this chapter on death at Tempe Beach. The closest call might have been a near electrocution in the fifties. Dan remembers a child climbing onto an electric car the concessionaire had provided under the awning by the snack bar and then grabbing the metal fence. Since the area was adjacent to the pool, the cement floor was wet, and the child received a powerful shock: "Joe [Spracale], I think it was Joe, and I pulled him off and gave him back pressure arm lift and we brought him around. So for the rest of the summer he and I were able to get drinks at the concession stand for five cents instead of ten or twenty cents. That was our reward."

Although Joe doesn't remember this rescue, he does recall another that happened just before he went on duty one day. As he was talking to some boys, their father dived into the pool just as a swimmer crossed his path: "In trying to avoid the boy he hit his head on the bottom of the pool. We floated him to the side of the pool keeping his neck straight and got him on a board in the water.... He wore a neck brace for awhile for a neck fracture."

Years later, Linda (Carnal) Whatley found herself in the same position as that swimmer, except that it was she, not the diver, who was hurt when as she surfaced, his head hit squarely on her nose:

"Someone had to pull me out of the water, then called my mom to take me to the doctor. My nose wasn't broken, but I recall the doc stuffed several yards of gauze up one nostril. I ended up with two black eyes which eventually turned yellow/green and a swollen nose. I was so embarrassed to go out in public for several weeks, but Dad said it was a badge of honor and I should not worry about it."

These injuries make clear why the cardinal rule of the swimming pool, second only to "No Running," was "No Swimming Under the Diving Boards." If a poolside dive could produce such harm, imagine what would happen if a diver from the high board were to land on someone underneath, or on the deck below, as one boy did when waiting for his turn to dive. As John Hollis, who was guarding that day, recalls : "He was leaning against the rail along the back of the board and somehow fell back and broke his collar bone." Instead of calling an ambulance or filling out forms to head off a lawsuit, John took care of the matter himself: "I just put him in my car and took him to Tempe Clinic, and he got all patched up."

Another legendary fall involved a boy who had been sat down by a lifeguard for misbehaving at the pool. Both the lifeguards Paul and Alex remember him, instead, climbing up a tree near the fence and then, when the branch broke beneath him, coming down on one of the river-stone columns interspersed among the fence's panels, made of black steel spikes. As Alex describes it, "We said, 'Oh, my God!' I don't know why he wasn't speared. He missed the fence by about that much and instead, I think, dislocated his arm."

Park Fence, circa 1934

On the whole, however, injuries at Tempe Beach were rare. The lifeguards whistled us into compliance and thus kept us safe. Today we can call up only minor ailments: bruises, burning feet, and punctures by bullheads on that long walk home. There was cherry toe: "something you could get when your feet weren't accustomed to pushing off the side of the pool" (Tom). There were bloodshot eyes and sunburns produced by a cloudless sky: "We would ride home with the worst sunburns in the world. My mom gave us tea baths to relieve them" (Joanie). There were still-lit cigarettes lying in wait for the bare feet of children in the snack bar line. There was cold, and hunger in the afternoons. But mostly there was fun, the fun that only youth and health and water could provide. And afterwards, resting on our towels in the sun, there was that story, told and retold but still mainly true (had there been a Snopes to rate it) of the man that drowned at Tempe Beach: Charles Thornberg, twenty years old, from West

Virginia, on April 25th, 1945, when he was sucked into the drain as he was NOT pool hopping at Tempe Beach, and did NOT thus bring on his own demise. His only fault was an ignorance of the vacuum effect in his decision to enter a draining pool and the giving nature that had drawn him in the first place to help out a friend.

How many times that friend must have rued his decision to correct so small a lapse: the early draining of the pool that night. The hour or two of swim time he'd envisioned lost must have paled against the lifetime lost in that drain. Had either acted differently, the drowned man or his lifeguard friend, Charles Thornberg might have lived to see that deadly drain made obsolete when the city tore down Tempe Beach. He would have then been thirty-nine, only one year younger than the pool where he instead would die, a pool that—without his plunge—might have made it forty years, its entire span, without a single drowning to its name.

Other Voices

Swimming for Tempe Beach
"Swallowing frogs' eggs during swim practice.
Yech!"

In 2012, nearly fifty years after the closing of
Tempe Beach, Eldon Smith's eyes tear up at the
mention of chlorine. "It happened to me yesterday too,"
he explains, "like a Pavlovian dog, you know." Swim
goggles had yet to be invented and everyone who
worked out in the mornings under Coaches Joe Spracale
(1951-54; 1957-60) or Marvin Williams (1961-63)
remembers biking home from practice "with blurry red
eyes stinging" (Cindy Statz Matoon). For Herb
McClure the hallmark of those bike rides home was the
haze that he peddled through, his eyes scarcely able to
see. Eldon, in fact, once collided with some stationary
object ("I forget now if it was a car or a tree"). Around
ten o'clock on summer mornings, when practice let out,
the town was a veritable movie-house cartoon, its
streets overrun by these Mr. Magoos.

The next day these same swimmers, eyes just
recovered, headed back toward the pool. Cindy
Mattoon admits she's unsure where the motivation lay,
what impelled her to rise so early on those summer days
and swim in third-day water, "very murky and full of
chlorine," not to mention cope with wind sprints which
were "killers," especially on the first day of practice
every year. These swimmers must have been, like their
coach Joe Spracale, all "water freaks." Chuck Holly is a
classic case: swimming, diving and guarding at Tempe

Beach, then moving west to do ocean swims and riptide rescues at Redondo Beach. Charlene (Mills)
Ashworth still remembers first encountering water at
age two or three when her uncle tossed her in, saying
"Sink or Swim!": "I must have taken to the water,
because I've loved it ever since."

Others seem hard-wired to compete. Elissa
(Montgomery) Tap remembers first discovering this
impulse in herself after lessons one year: "Participants
were lined up maybe six or eight abreast and asked to
swim the width of the pool. I remember swimming as
hard and as fast as I could, for some reason discovering
a competitive streak in myself." Cindy and Chuck's
brother Alan must have shared this trait. Both
eventually signed on with professional coaches to
improve their times. Still at Tempe Beach, Eldon relied
on this killer's instinct to boost his chances at the end of
a race:

"I tended to push myself really hard if I was
swimming anchor on a relay team, and I remember one
time swimming over in Mesa when I was really pushing
to beat the other guy to the edge of the pool. I ended up
knocking myself out. It was just for a brief period of
time that I was under water. And I remember John
Southern, who was really quite a swimmer, he and
several other people brought me home."

Whatever their motive, many young Tempeans
traded sleeping in on summer mornings for biking cross
town to the pool. A kind of team spirit must have built
along the way. As Elissa describes it: "The number of
bicyclists grew as we picked up members who lived on
the way, arriving at the pool in a gang." Once there,

Cindy recalls the gate left open for the children on the team. Sometimes the water would still be flowing from the pipe attached to the fire hydrant, and so the team would swim in the "fresh, freezing water as it poured into the body of the 50-meter pool." Sometimes the swimmers would arrive before the coach, climb the fence, and jump in nonetheless, some of them, like Alan, diving for coins at the bottom of the pool: "In the morning the pool would be very clear because all the sediment would drop to the bottom. Because of the angle of the sun you could see the reflection of the coins, and so that was the first thing I'd do: go down to the bottom of the pool, and then I'd have my money for the day." One morning, however, the Parks and Recreation Director had an early-morning meeting and saw, as he crossed the bridge, a pool full of children, completely unsupervised, down below. After that, Alan said, the "boom came down, and we never did it again."

Once the coach arrived, the workout began: slow and steady circuits from the deep end to the shallow end and back again; sprints punctuated with flip turns just shy of the wall; racing dives. The team, out-of-shape from the long school year, had only a week or two before the opening meet in early June. Alan remembers having no idea that his competition had been prepping all year for a meet that would find him barely out of school and up against the Dick Smith Swim Gym—formidable swimmers at the top of their game: "We were competing, unbeknownst to most of us dumb kids (we had no idea the others were swimming year round) so we were competing after having had two or three weeks of training and when it got to the middle of the summer six, seven weeks of practice."

The coaches, however, had this variance in mind, devising low-tech methods for closing such a gap. As Elissa recalls, Joe Spracale would condition his team by making them swim with their tennis shoes on. When the shoes finally came off, she felt like "a powerful fish," hardly disadvantaged by her team's limitations: seasonal swimming, volunteer coaches, and murky water that burned the eyes. As the swim coach in 1956, Coach Emil Kass devised another system for developing strength. He had pulleys installed in a wall so that, supine on a table, the swimmers could strengthen their backs and arms. Beyond that, their equipment was as basic as its name. According to Alan:

We really had kick *boards*. Today they still call them kick boards though they're made of styrofoam or they're made of plastic, but ours were boards, wooden boards, two-by-sixes—two two-by-sixes about eighteen inches long. And then there was another two-by-two, maybe two-by-four across, both ends nailed or screwed down and painted with aquatic paint."

The team had no goggles, no caps, no fins for workouts, no pull buoys for building upper body strength. There was no weight training and so few swimmers that making up a relay in the various age groups was a challenge in itself. In fact, Daf remembers Chuck once making us swim— completely unconditioned divers—to fill some need of the swimming team.

And yet Tempe Beach swam as full a schedule as that of any year-round team. In 1958, coached by Joe

Spracale, they swam at both Junior and Senior AAU meets, at the Junior Olympics, at the Roosevelt Relays, at dual meets, at three-way meets, at meets as far away as Tucson, at meets where as many as eight teams competed, and of course at their own home meets every year. The *Tempe Daily News* kept close watch on their progress, printing front-page articles, often with pictures, and detailed tallies of the final team points.

In the summer of '58, for example, the paper announced the first home meet of the year with a picture of Tempe's twenty-three swimmers, some climbing the ladder of the highboard, others sitting on the board. Standing beside the ladder in a group of six swimmers are young males with washboard abs, a testament to those wind sprints and long, slow laps swum with sneaker-bound feet. One month later, in July, it ran a page-one shot of a men's freestyle start at the State Junior AAU trials. The swimmers stretch out in old-school racing-dive form. In the background is the Tempe Beach Snack Bar sign reading ROOT BEER/ HOT DOG. That same year a small group of swimmers, about to set off for a Tucson meet, holds a green and gold banner made by Mrs. Wilford Lewis. Beside the team stands "coach of the touring squad" Joe Spracale with his iconic James Bond chest. As late as August 24th the team was still competing, though school must have just begun. A photo shows Candy Lewis and Eldon Smith holding high-point trophies won that weekend in Prescott: Eldon's for 13-14 year-old boys, Candy's for 12 and under girls.

Swim Team 1958

Beach-hosted AAU Meet

Off to Tucson

Candy and Eldon

Sometimes articles highlighted swimmers, as when Eldon and Chuck "combined to bring the beachers all their points," at a mid-July meet at the Roosevelt Pool, or when Tempe Beach's Candy Lewis was the sole girl entered for the Tempe team. Other names appeared whenever Tempe garnered points: Dave Carraway, Jack McCracken, Herb McClure, Roger Worseley, Jerry Anderson, Robert Horton, John Southern; and for the girls' team Elissa Montgomery, Ramona and Eleanor Lee, Pat Conley, Jackie Herren.

In the summer of '62, under coach Marvin Williams, the team was still as active as ever, the paper still attentive to the swimmers' feats. An article in May called the team back to practice before school had even let out, with swimmers meeting at 4:30 daily, eight a.m. on Saturdays. The article also laid out the summer's schedule: the Saguaro meet, May 26-27; the Junior and Senior AAU meets; the short and long-course Junior Olympics; the Southern Arizona Invitational; the Northern Arizona Open; and the Arizona Relays, to be held June 5th at the ASU pool. To prepare for the latter, Marv staged an intra-squad competition where eleven swimmers would be chosen for this meet. When the paper printed the Relays results, it found the team's performance "highly creditable," given its barely two weeks of training as compared to the year-round sessions of the swimmers it came up against: Alan Holly placed fifth in the hundred-yard freestyle, while Cindy Statz and John Townsend took sixths in that same event in the 13-14 age group. Another sixth-place medal went to the boy's 13-14 200-meter freestyle relay team, comprised of Steve and John Townsend, Dave Mumbaugh, and Larry Peralta.

Later in June the same names show up in the meet results, an AAU age-group meet in Mesa; another at the Scottsdale pool. By July the team will have traveled twice to Tucson, once taking Cindy, Alan, and Charlene Mills to an AAU meet, the next time entering these three as well as Becky Dycus, Larry Peralta, and Dick Vihel in the Junior Olympic Short Course there. The Tempe Beach-hosted AAU meet will fill up pages when it's held here in early July. Dick Smith Swim Gym's Bill Mettler will set a new meet record with his 59-second 100-meter freestyle time, then share his front-page picture with Randy Brodersen of Phoenix, who was second, and the Beach's own Alan who came in third. At this point in the summer, Cindy and Alan are grabbing headlines: "Holly, Statz Shine For Tempe Beach in Swim Meeting." The end of the season finds them smiling from a front-page photo as the year's outstanding swimmers. Flanking them are Gabrielle Dolphin and Carlos Molina, most improved girl and boy.

Carlos, Alan, Cindy, and Gabrielle

Though these articles catalogue the team's activities, they hardly capture the flavor of those meets, where the competition was often but the context for a summer's fun. Perhaps the team's very status as underdog helped the swimmers bond as they waited for their races and then again for the final contests later in the day. An easy companionship seems to have prevailed. As Cindy recalls: "We'd show up to those meets, spread our towels together and share orange slices, each of us with our own "honey bears" to suck on for energy."

Alan confirms both the team's cohesion and the fun they had in describing a memorable Tucson meet. Instead of resting up between the heats and the finals, the team instead descended on their hotel pool: "A local TV or radio station was there interviewing a then-popular group called the Ink Spots by the water. So now you have about twenty kids going off the diving board and doing cherry bombs, just turning the place into chaos." To contain that energy, Coach Marv took them to a movie. After this restful interlude the team received an unusual pre-race instruction: "Don't tell anyone I took you to this movie!" As Alan explains: "Movies weren't rated then, but movies weren't all that bad to begin with. This movie would have been more tame than any TV program today. But in those days it was not tame," hence Marvin's angst. Cindy remembers that movie trip too and the culprit as perhaps a Jerry Lewis film.

Driving down to Tucson was a treat in itself, especially for young boys enamored of cars. Eldon remembers riding in Elissa's dad's blue woody Pontiac, a definite collector's item today. Herb McClure reminded Eldon of an earlier time when they drove to Tucson in a '55 Plymouth wearing blue terry panchos provided for the team. The most vivid memory for Eldon is riding to a meet on a rainy day in Coach Kass's Model A Ford: "One thing I remember is there was a big puddle, and we hit it. It just so happened there was a guy coming from the other direction; we just completely saturated his whole windshield, so we got a big kick out of that, though Coach Kass was a little bit embarrassed." Coming back from meets was fun as well. As Eldon recalls: "Joe had a budget, and he used to treat us to some good meals afterwards."

Even the bad times seem to have been good, or at least recounted with the same animation that accompanied depictions of the happy times. An email from Tom Ditsworth, for example, cites a drawback of training in an old-fashioned pool: " Swallowing frogs' eggs during swim practice. Yech!" Though funny on its own, Tom's comment made me roar in light of a remark made by Alex Arredondo just weeks before: "I remember Marv Williams grew up right next to Tempe Beach or close by, and he'd go to the river bottom, get some frogs, and turn them loose at Tempe Beach." Little did the child-Marvin realize his own contribution to a future of frogs' eggs tormenting swimmers he himself would coach two decades hence.

The worst time for Eldon must have been 1959 when, sidelined by mononucleosis, he missed out on most of the meets. Yet even then Eldon overachieved, his spirits intermittently high: "I'd be out a week or two and then I would come in and swim on the relay team—I'd knock myself out to swim—and then I'd be out a week or two, then come back and do the same thing." For him there seems to have been no middle ground, no golden mean. When not churning full-throttle though the water he was idling at home: "That month I didn't have the energy to strum my guitar."

In addition to sharing their highs and lows, without my prompting almost all the swimmers volunteered the names of former teammates, fondly remembered after all this time. Charlene mentioned Candy Lewis, Cindy Statz, Margaret Winsor, and Eleanor Lee, adding to these female teammates Chuck and Alan Holly ("I had a crush on both"). Eldon remembers Pat Southern and Pat Connolly, in addition to her brother John. He still recalls a medley relay team comprised of Craig Thompson, Dave Carraway, Jerry Anderson and Jack McCracken ("I think they had a state record") in the late fifties. Cindy recalls Alan and Chuck Holly, Eldon

Smith, R. C. Rover, David Mumbaugh, Margaret Winsor, Charlene Mills, Carlos Molina (and more!)." The last two names on Alan's list overlap with hers: Cindy, Candy Lewis, John Townsend, Dick Vihel, the Horton brothers, R. C. Rover and David Mumbaugh. That last name, David Mumbaugh, a friend to both and, as Alan remembers him, a "very nice person," put the swim team on the map when he ended up murdering an ASU coed three blocks from the swimming pool in 1966.

I can still see the headlines of the *Tempe Daily News* that day, and the picture of the victim staring out at me. Laura Bernstein was small and dark with long, straight hair like mine and gold hoop earrings like the ones I wore. She'd been stabbed while locking up her bike behind the Casa Loma on Mill and Fourth, her fate overnight destroying the innocence of old Tempe. I remember the reaction at school that day: "Well, we don't know who did it, but we sure know the motive. He thought it was you!" For months I slept with my bedroom door locked.

Alan remembers the details of the story: that it was David, then eighteen, who ran to the police and reported the body, and later, when the police department figured it out, David who admitted having wanted since the eighth grade to murder someone. Laura Bernstein's sister, Jane, reveals the rest in her 2000 memoir titled *Bereft*. David, she tells us, had been tripped up by his own inconsistencies when the police called him back for repeated interviews. First he said he'd been going to work when he stopped to see a Dodge in the Dana Brothers lot. He had driven past Third by mistake and parked on Fourth, then discovered the body as he walked down the block, attracted by the beam from Laura's flashlight on the ground. Out of breath, his pants torn from the fall he took when running to the station, he told the police he'd found a girl he thought was dead. He'd left her, he said, with some friends.

But as time wore on, those "friends" became strangers who lived in apartments nearby. David had found a girl who'd "been murdered," he told these strangers, not one he "thought was dead" as he'd been coming home from, not going to, work. The flashlight by her body was off, not on. He'd discovered the body not because of that flashlight's beam, but because his foot had "kind of hit her" as he passed by in the dark. A detective remembers David breaking out in "the damnedest sweat" as he heard himself losing control of his tale. When they asked him to bring in the clothes he'd been wearing that night, he gave them a white shirt, not the plaid one he'd worn to the station. His shoes had on them what appeared to be blood. Though David was probably in already too deeply to recover, he sealed his fate when he noticed a switchblade on an officer's desk and said, "You found it! How did you do that? I threw it into the canal at 48th Street." When the city then dredged the canal with a magnet, they recovered Mumbaugh's identical knife, the one he had used to stab Laura Bernstein "four times in the body and twice in the head."

Had Jane Bernstein not made those visits to Tempe, first to learn the details of her sister's fate, then to be present at the commutation hearings, Mumbaugh might have been given parole. Instead, she convinced the board that he might kill again, her evidence the comment that he made to the police on the very night that knife caught his eye: "I had that feeling again tonight of wanting to get hold of someone and beat the hell out of them."

Mumbaugh died in jail when he was forty-five, after taking from a picture frame a long, slender shard of glass and puncturing his heart. More frightening to me than either the murder or the suicide is imagining the thoughts that must have cycled through his mind as he churned through the water at those early morning practices—back and forth— the long, slow movement of his limbs unloosing those repellent thoughts while his teammates swam along beside.

No dark deed exists to discredit the coaches who paced the deck while Mumbaugh swam; quite the contrary. Both Joe and Marvin were father figures to those they coached. Joe, in fact, refers to the swimmers as "my kids—Elissa, Candy, Eldon, Chuck," and the kids return the compliment: "I really looked up to him, almost as a father," Chuck reveals. It was Joe who advanced Chuck's love of the water by saying to the fifth grade student in the class where he was practice teaching, 'Hey, Charlie, come on down to the swimming pool this summer, and you can be on the swim team.'" Years later it would be Joe at the wheel when Chuck traveled down to the Tucson meets, and Joe who once arranged for Chuck to stay overnight with his brother there so he could swim both days of the meet.

Charlene remembers Joe as being very strict at practice, but also encouraging them to do their best. Not surprisingly Elissa tells me, "Every memory I have of Joe is a happy one." His devotion to kids extended beyond the members of the team. Daf, for example, says that "Mr. Spracale," her fourth grade teacher, "meant the world to me." His care extended outward to the town as well. Even after the dark days of segregation at Tempe Beach, some Mexican-Americans were leery of the swimming pool. "We had to make them feel welcome," Joe said, since there still were "people entrenched in that stuff." Joe would recruit these neighborhood kids to be on the team, enticing them with year-long passes to the pool.

Marvin continued this tradition. "A lot of the kids were Mexican American," he told me, adding "At one point I probably had the best Mexican-American swimming team—summer team—around." Memories of Marvin's inclusiveness, however, are inseparable from those of his physique. Tom Ditsworth, for example, concurred with my allusion to the toon that first appeared Marv's second year as coach of the team (*Marvel Comics*, May, 1962): "Yes, he looked like the Hulk, 'ceptin not green." I don't think we kids had known a body builder before we met Marv. We were mesmerized. Frank Downey describes him as "so heavily muscled that when he tried to scratch his head his shoulder muscles got in the way." Elissa remembers him as "short and stout" but most importantly as "kind." For Tom Ditsworth he was a "good guy....who never took off his dark sunglasses." Behind those glasses was a man who probably never knew how important he had been in his swimmers' lives. Frank Downey says it best:

"[Marv] was one of those grown ups who just appeared in our lives, had great influence, and went away to his private life when he was done. I don't remember his last name. I was always too shy to engage him in conversation, but he inspired us to have fun, work hard, and do our best. Some years we were really competitive, some years not so much. Winning and losing never seemed very important."

Fifty years after Marvin's last practice in August, 1963, the Tempe Beach swimmers still cherish their medals, their ribbons and their memories. One, Alan Holly, still swims today, "a lonely sport, but as long as I enjoy it and can do it, I think I will." That he still "can do it" is an understatement. In the summer of 2012 he went to Nationals, placing fourth in the 65-69 age group's two-hundred meter freestyle. Of his three children one has the swimming bug too, as well as the drive that made Elissa turn a swim lesson into a contest and Eldon to literally knock himself out. She swims year round today, specializing in the butterfly. Her father Alan knows only too well why: "Once when she was little, she asked me what the hardest stroke was, and I said the butterfly. Without knowing it, I laid down the gauntlet."

The Synchronized Swim Team
"Knee up, leg straight, point your toes."

Synchronized Swimmers at Tempe Beach

Getting dressed on summer mornings, to the children of Tempe, meant putting on a swim suit. For Margaret (Winsor) Maciborka it meant keeping in rotation a series of three: one for swim-team practice at eight, another for dive-team practice with Glen Jones after lunch, and a third for nighttime practice with the synchronized swimmers back at Tempe Beach. Margaret was an overachiever. When she was only seven, she took up swimming in response to a doctor's demand that they find some way to open up her bronchial tubes. Margaret, now asthma-free, took the doctor at his word, biking to the pool from her home at Sixth and Maple, then tripling that regimen by joining three teams. Even in the halls of Tempe High, well after the pool had been closed for the season, Wendy Cole remembers Margaret with her swimming-pool hair, "always shiny and faintly green." She was diving year-round on that private team.

The synchronized swimmers also practiced in the mornings, as early as six-thirty, so to free up the pool for the swim team by eight. It is hard to imagine many girls being willing to arrive at that hour to swim on the team. But in 1962 seventeen girls aged ten to sixteen both joined and persisted to showcase their skills at a Tempe Beach performance at the end of July. Millie Loughrige, who created the team in 1960 only two months after she'd arrived in town, still remembers these swimmers—Margaret, in addition to the others—and "the hard work they did." The girls, in turn, remember her, the young coach from Iowa who, fresh out of high school, was "our big Sis." As Margaret, however, is quick to add, Millie ran a tight ship. At those early-morning practices they started with conditioning—four sets each of the crawl, the breast stroke, and the backstroke across the pool—then continued on with treading water to build the strength their stunts required. The girls also needed the breath-holding power to complete their routines, which in turn required mastery of "those crazy nose plugs," a process Linda (Carnal) Whatley called "a learning experience in itself."

Mastering the various stunts, some basic, some more involved, took up most of the time at those early-morning sessions. Even today Nancy (Leach) Lesko finds herself reverting to the default setting established by Millie all those years ago: "I still go into the plank-type float with the hand-motion [sculling]...on the rare occasions I'm in the water." Mary Jane (Wegner) Torok remembers too a classic move, the ballet leg—"knee up, leg straight, point your toes"— and the more elaborate "submarine": "You'd put one leg up, then go under water until just your foot and ankle were out, and come back up." (It might have been this very move—the submarine—with its spotlight on the pointed toe that inspired those burlesques Daf and I enacted at about that time). She also remembers a stunt performed with a group aligned into a human chain: "If you had a lot of people you could line up three or four, then put your feet around their necks, arch your back, and do a big backwards somersault," pulling everyone under and then back up.

Valerie McMillion recalls Linda doing the more difficult moves, the Flamingo and the Eiffel Tower, both beginning with the ballet leg, but then adding turns, underwater rotations and even a second extended leg. Yet Valerie herself must have been quite adept: like Millie before her, she became a Naiad, a synchronized swimmer at ASU. Still everyone agrees that Margaret was "the star," "very natural in the water," and thus not only garnering solos, but "winning everything, she was so good."

These winnings took place at pools around the valley— at country clubs, at Perry Pool in Phoenix, and once, as Millie recalls, at a pool in Glendale that she set off for with the team in tow: "I drove all the way to Glendale, and I got on Grand Avenue, which terrified me because it's just so different than the other streets, you know. You're going on a diagonal. But we made it there all right and then, thank heavens, back again." Not only did Millie chauffeur her team, she provided their music (old-fashioned records cranked up loud), organized the swimmers into solos and duets, helped with their costumes, and choreographed the girls' routines. In addition, she sometimes judged the meets, giving points for the theme, choreography and synchronization, that "they're keeping the tempo, all of them at once." To manage that, the girls had not only to count but to "watch the leader under water, since you couldn't hear the music that well." At times a pool would have underwater speakers, but mostly they relied on that counting instead, "over and over," as Millie put it: "You just had it in your head."

If the sport was collaborative, so was the process by which costume and music selections were made. "We used to debate," as Linda recalls, "over and over about song selections." The choice that sticks in her mind is that of "Autumn Leaves." Valerie remembers that song too, along with the "twirling fingers" that were part of the routine. Mothers and daughters, according to Margaret, would pool their talents to come up with outfits for the various numbers. The girls had sashes and tear-away skirts that they'd drop on the deck before entering the pool. They often had some kind of headdress, as Millie remembers, to coordinate their look. Sometimes the girls just borrowed their costumes, as Mary Jane did when she needed a white suit: "It was really uncomfortable, but I had to have it for that show." Other times they created their own, as when Margaret paired a white suit with a black cap she'd glittered herself, then swam to the music of Tchaikovsky's "Swan Lake." And Millie sewed too.

It is easy to see why synchronized swimming was such a draw, appealing as it did to the female preference for a group dynamic. Its hybrid nature must have lured girls too, mixing swimming with the culture of the dance recital and a smattering of arts and crafts. Margaret, for example, can remember doing "deck work" (rehearsing their musical performances on land) before repeating the sequences in the pool: "You had to allow for the slower movements in the water." The resulting performance might not be intended for a swim meet at all, but for an exhibition, delighting an audience with sheer display.

A perfect example is the "show on water," held July 24, 1962, at Tempe Beach, then repeated the next night at Mesa Country Club. The seventeen-girl team presented "Swimming the Year Round," by interpreting the moods, as the newspaper puts it, of the various months. The program opened with the full team, in red and white suits, arranging themselves into a Valentine's Day heart. The next month, March, was represented by the melody "Wild is the Wind," and the swimming of Margaret Winsor, Linda Carnal, Nancy Leach and Louise Vogel. "April in Portugal" provided the music for a ten-girl routine, with six of those same girls evoking Fall in a number swum to "Autumn Leaves." "White Christmas," a trio performance by Margaret Windsor, Laura Sellards and Louise Vogel, brought out the feeling of the year's last month, while Margaret and Millie performed solo routines. Millie interpreted August in her program swum to "Summertime," while Margaret called up June with Mancini's "Moon River."

Cited in the next day's paper as a highlight of the first-night's show is October's spook routine "The Twilight Zone" with Mary Lehto, Nancy Leach, Mary Jane Wegner and Linda Carnal. Also mentioned is the comic duet performed by Louise Vogel and Laura Sellards, two "Young at Heart" hobos, who captured the mood of July. Singled out too are both the opening number and the grand finale, where seventeen girls swam to "Moments to Remember," their bodies at the end spelling out TEMPE.

Reading these accounts makes me marvel at the sheer logistics of pulling that show off, especially considering the challenge of coaching girls as skilled as Margaret along with those as young as ten. In fact, just two weeks earlier Millie had taken those young girls to Madison School for a Junior Stunt Meet, where Starr Sellards won the 10-and-Under age group for her execution of five separate stunts while Connie Carlson placed third among those aged 11-12.

Even more commanding is the atmosphere those articles create, the picture that emerges of the pool itself, in its next-to-last season, as a festive, still-communal spot. An estimated two-hundred seventy five people watched the girls perform that night, "one of the best audience turnouts yet." The water would have sparkled under the lights where the Beach community pooled its efforts to help out Millie, one of their own. Elissa from the swim team narrated the show. Our coach Chuck joined "The Flying Nincompoops" to clown dive during the intermission. Both, of course, would be back at the pool the next morning at eight.

The synchronized swimmers, perhaps more than members of any other team, expressed to me the "huge fun" they had at those meets, exhibitions, and day-and-nighttime practices—the camaraderie that somehow grew despite the "stair-step" of ages comprising the team. Perhaps the need to synchronize their movements in the water carried over to the way they behaved on shore. They were groomed to harmonize, rather than compete—at their meets and exhibitions, at the pot-luck picnics they held in the park, at their end-of-season gathering to pass out awards. Linda still remembers the pride she felt when, her second year, she received a trophy as the Most Improved Swimmer: "I kept that trophy for thirty years, then finally tossed it during my last move." Valerie remembers wanting for her own child that feeling of accomplishment, "that great camaraderie," as well as the fun, but McClintock had no synchronized team. Today she is thankful at least to have had herself the resource that was Tempe Beach—and more importantly the model that was Millie: "She gave us the experience."

Guarding at Tempe Beach
"Nothing. We're cleaning the pool."

While the lifeguards watched us leaping from the high-board, floating in our inner tubes, and plunging after dibble-sticks, we, too, watched them. We marked their slow rotation to new sentry points around the pool. We turned our heads when their whistles blew. We knew their names. We saw the deep red of their swim trunks fade progressively from May to June until late in August these sentinels—these macho men—would be garbed in pink.

What we didn't know was the work they did apart from sitting and standing and watching us, the long hours they toiled (at a dollar an hour) to maintain the pool where in turn we swam. Even before the free-swim day that opened the pool, they had begun their work. As Dan Arredondo recalls: "We'd start early, we were still in school, and we'd have to paint the pool, paint the bottom, paint the black lines to get it ready every year. And I remember that bridge across [between the main pool and the slide pool]. We'd put this non-skid stuff on; we'd use rollers. We had to get our sunglasses on because the reflection was so bright."

Neither did we understand the labor involved in maintaining a pool that, without a filter, needed heavy chlorine. Chuck explains how that chlorine was dispersed, through narrow pipes inside the pool: "I don't know if you remember. They were pretty camouflaged, but if you were in the water and you put your foot by them you could feel a little bit of water coming out, and that water was infused with chlorine gas." Eldon Smith, who guarded in the sixties, claims his least-favorite duty was preparing these pipes before the pool's high season got underway. His memory of the task is inseparable from that of his body, permeated by cold: "The thing that I liked least was just before Memorial Day your job was to take a hammer and a nail and open up the chlorine holes. And every time you hit that nail you knew—well I would try to dodge the water—you knew it would be cold." One's knowledge of these pipes would come in handy when the county inspectors arrived at the Beach. Dan Arredondo explains why the pool would always ace that test: "They'd come down here and they'd give us a flask. They'd want us to go down where the water was deep. So we'd go down there right where the water [with the chlorine gas] was coming out and bring it back up. And they'd say, 'Great! Pass!'"

The chlorine itself was housed in a shack on the north side of the pool, its smell still recalled by the lifeguards who entered there to change the tank. Chuck, to this day, recoils at the smell of Clorox, its scent reminiscent of the times when, attaching a new bottle, "you didn't get the threads just right," and the gas would escape. Paul Aldridge, who guarded at the pool from 1955 to 1961, often wonders if the breathing problems he has today could have stemmed from the chlorine in that shed, a chemical whose power becomes all-too apparent in a harrowing memory of lifeguard John Hollis:

"One time Don [Wilkinson] and I were changing the bottles, which were delivered back at the northwest side of the pool, and they'd just sit out there in the sun.

And then we would roll them—they were really heavy—we'd roll them across the rocks and then hook them up, take the old tube off, and put the new tube on. One day we got a little careless, I guess, and Don and I got a snoot full of chlorine, and it actually put both of us down just briefly."

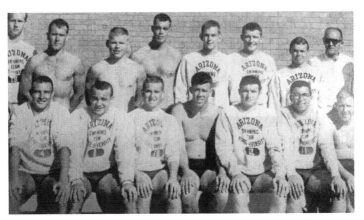

Front row: Eldon Smith second from left, Chuck Holly fifth from left, Allen Adams fourth from left back row

Even more dangerous than handling those tanks was draining the pool—three times a week—since the power of that suction could trap a swimmer as it did so tragically in 1945. Since then the lifeguards took extra care when cleaning the pool, with two guards on duty from nine o'clock when the drain was opened until nearly eleven when the filling began. As Dan tells it, everyone wanted to work those nights: "We were open ten to nine. It was a long day. And then we'd get another couple of hours for draining the pool." In addition to the extra pay, there was always money at the bottom of the pool. Joe Spracale got his start as a teen helping clean the pool, with the money on the bottom becoming his pay. Later, according to Marvin Williams, the guards simply divvied it up, while Chuck remembers saving the money in a jar until the summer's end, when it would fund steak dinners for all at Monti's just across the street.

There was more than money at the bottom of the pool. There were bobby pins, band-aids, unmentionable objects, and mounds of hair. As the water drained out into the park, the lifeguards hosed down this debris, sometimes using push brooms as well and occasionally, to combat algae, a brush and a can of HTH. John Hollis details this routine:

"We'd start draining the pool. We'd clean out the bath houses, and it would take about a half hour for the water to get down so that the shallow end was exposed. Then we'd take fire hoses and we'd chase the water down the rest of the way. It probably took a good hour and a half to drain the pool. Then, after having cleaned it all out, we would shut the gate again, and then we'd set up this big pipe, attached to the fire hydrant, which was about ten or fifteen feet off the side of the pool, and it took all night to fill it up."

After a dust storm Don Wilkinson remembers it taking "forever" to clean the pool with guards staying there until one or two a.m. They might have, earlier, closed down the pool because of lightning when the storm rolled in. This didn't, however, mean the guards went home. Both Don and Chuck remember having, instead, a field day with the pool to themselves—lightning be damned— as they sprang from the diving boards, buffeted by wind.

The guards cleaned the bath house the same way they cleaned the pool, by simply hosing down its cement floors and river-rock walls. Both Chuck and John made sure to mention that the girls' side was dirtier than the boys', their smugness never challenged by the explanation that came quickly to my mind. (Perhaps the boys were peeing in the pool.) All that remained, then, was hosing out the baby pool and, with those same hoses, filling it back up.

This rote to-do list hardly captures the pleasures of those nights, any more than the prospect of extra pay accounts for the clamor to work this shift. Of course, the pool was beautiful at night. As Millie recalls, "The sky was dark; the lights were on." It was a festive setting, but even more so when one factors in the girls. Dan's narration says it all:

"We'd close the doors and turn on the lights, and we'd turn on the jukebox. Sometimes we had ladies come around and help us clean the pool. And some people would see that and they'd call the city. [When we got the call asking what was going on] we'd say, 'Nothing, we're cleaning the pool.' Then we'd turn the lights out and swim around while the pool was filling up."

For two years John worked this shift with the woman who would be his wife, their dates hardly action-packed—the aquatic equivalent of watching paint dry—but romantic still in the presence of what Joe Spracale called "champagne water" and, overhead, the summer sky:

"Once we got the water started and were filling the pool, we would go over to Monti's and we would buy hamburgers, and hamburgers then were a dollar twenty-five, big old juicy half-pound hamburgers with fries. Even though a few of us, in fact most of us, were under-aged, a few of us would somehow wrangle a six-pack of beer, and we'd sit there and watch the pool start to fill up—drink a beer or two and eat some hamburgers. That was my wife's—our— courtship, two nights a week for two years."

Even without the girls, the draining process could be a blast, quite literally, when armed with a hose. In addition to using them to spray each other, the lifeguards turned them on the fig-eater beetles that inhabited the river bed and came flying out of there on draining nights, attracted by the lights and the empty pool. Their presence transformed Tempe Beach into a kind of arcade with the lifeguards engaging in an early version of Space Invaders. As John describes it: "On occasion we'd put one lifeguard up in the chair kind of watching for the beetles, and he would tell the lifeguard down in the pool with the hose which way to shoot. 'Three o'clock!' 'Six o'clock!' We'd pull them out of the sky."

All these descriptions of twice and three-times weekly drainings made me question my memory of fourth and even fifth-day waters when my friends and I swam at Tempe Beach, water so opaque that the lane lines vanished beneath it, as did our bodies and our popsicle sticks. It was Alex who finally explained this discrepancy, his memory confirmed by newspaper stories from the early sixties in the *Tempe Daily News*: "There was a time when I was a lifeguard that there was a water shortage in Tempe, so the fire chief would call down and say, 'You cannot drain the pool.' We only had one tank up on the butte. And he'd say, 'If we have a fire it's going to burn everything down.'" Sure enough, on July 16, 1963, the paper reports on a large drop in water pressure—the second in less than a month—created by the double-whammy of a heat-wave and on-going drought.

Marvin remembers this water shortage too; in fact, he recalls once a whole week elapsing with no emptying of the pool. "So what we did, we would go down about every twenty minutes or so in the ten foot end with a mask on and, you know, feel around and make sure nobody was there. You really couldn't see all the way down." John concurs, adding that at times the pool became so murky that they'd shut down the deep end "and have three or four lifeguards swim the width of the pool on the bottom, just feeling around and hoping there wasn't a body there." I don't think we children understood the hazards of these times, so focused were we on our burning eyes. And, of course, our parents never had a clue. On the bright side, our steeping in fifth-day water made even more glorious the mornings when, at last, it gave way to first.

Only once do I remember arriving at practice with this first-day water pouring out from the pipe. Others remember this happening more often. Marvin frequently arrived with the pool still filling through the pipe that had been gushing (unmonitored) all through the night: "I used to dive right over that. It'd give you a little shot out." According to Chuck, sometimes the swim-team members and early-shift lifeguards would jump in and swim against the current "as the last few thousands of gallons flowed." These swimmers thus intuited the concept of the Endless Pool (or Counter-Current Pool) so popular today.

Front row: Joe Spracale far left, Marvin Williams far right, Roger Worseley (with white towel)

It must have been exhausting to work late draining the pool, then arrive at eight to coach a team—even worse when swimming lessons started and every guard pulled double shifts. That Tempe Beach should offer lessons to its citizens had been decreed some thirty years before, when the CCC camp enrollees, those who had built the bathhouse and the long, low surrounding walls out of rocks from the riverbed, were themselves consigned to swim classes during the week. In fact, in the 1930s Tempe Beach became the first venue in Arizona for "Red Cross sponsored aquatic school." Alex remembers people lining up for this free instruction: beginning classes, intermediate classes, advanced classes as well as classes for adults that were held at night. To get the message out, as he recalls, "We used the *Tempe Daily News*. We put coupons in there, "Free Swim Classes," whichever you wanted, and people signed up for the various times. I don't think we had limits. We were mobbed the whole time." In addition, there were Water Safety Instructor classes and the newly instituted Learn to Dive.

John describes an assembly-line method of instructing non-swimmers, some two hundred Tempe kids at a time. The ones new to swimming would start out in the shallow end just playing in the water, then learn to blow bubbles. Once they accomplished that, they'd move on to the second group, now readied for the floating stage. Each stage was allotted twenty minutes; then the whistles would blow. The life-guards would decide who had learned, for example, how to float and would thus move on. The sinkers would repeat the lesson with the group moving up from the bubble-blowing stage. Then: "The third stage was hanging onto the side with your face in the water and kicking. So now you're teaching the kicking part of the swimming fundamentals. In the fourth stage you're kicking and stroking, and the fifth stage was learning to breathe under your shoulder." After this final stage, all that remained was graduation with its penny and goldfish hunts and the requisite swimming across the pool.

Alex Arredondo

Alex hardly overstates the role of the lifeguards in water-proofing an entire town—"I think we taught most of Tempe to swim at that time"— a huge swath of people who remember, in addition to the freezing water, the words of encouragement that spurred them on. JoAnn (Voss) Brown can still hear Alex saying, "Come on, Joann. You can do it. You can do it." John's sister Janice (Hollis) Strickland is one of the few who learned so well that she actually caught a goldfish and received a prize: "A silver dollar. Real silver too. I still have it."

Goldfish Catchers, Far Left: Janice Hollis, Far Right: Randy Gill

On the other hand, no formal graduation was held for the swimmers in the life-saving class. One year, perhaps in response to this omission, the graduates created their own event, a darker version of the ice-chest dump on a winning coach by his football team. As Paul Aldridge tells it, "I was on the side of the pool, congratulating the students for successfully completing the class when they all rushed me, pushed me into the pool and then came in after me." Every time he surfaced to take a breath, another one would dunk him until "I seriously needed a breath and had to get rough with them." In those moments of critical oxygen debt, Paul envisioned the headlines of the next day's paper: "Lifeguard Drowns at Tempe Beach," with maybe a subtitle playing up the irony, "Students Had Just Finished Life-Saving Course."

The bulk of the lifeguards' time, however, was spent in their chairs, or standing by the baby pool, or roving when, on Sundays for example, the pool was "body-to-body people. You couldn't move" (Joe). There might be, in addition to the rover, as many as four or five other guards. Dan remembers one such day when the roving guard reported on a topless woman lying out on the lawn: "He told me 'She's completely exposed. She has no top on.' And I said 'Are you sure? I'll check it out.' Sure enough. I said, 'Ma'am, you can't do that.' She said, 'Why not? I do it at home.' (She was European.) And I said 'We don't do that,' so she covered up." On the way back to his post, then, Dan would hear what was clearly a first in the annals of Tempe Beach: the sound of a lifeguard being booed.

A more typical day was one of routine vigilance, especially at the trouble spots around the pool. The most dangerous area, according to Marvin, was the baby pool: "The worst thing, the thing we had to be careful of, was parents putting their kids in the baby pool and then walking off." For Alex it was the area sometimes marked by a rope, where the shallow waters became gradually deep: "The younger kids would go in and creep along the ledge into the sloping area, then get in over their heads." John considered rough-housers the ones to watch, wherever they might choose to swim: "We got our share of trouble makers. I'm not going to name names because some of them are still around, but there were some pretty difficult kids, and they wouldn't pay attention to any of the rules."

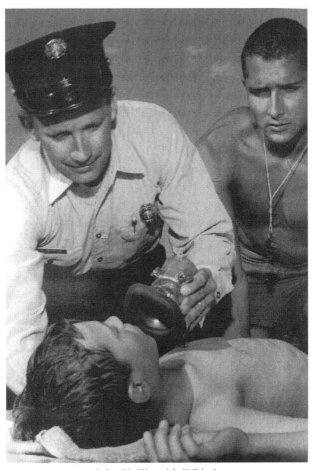
John Hollis with Whistle

The strategy for dealing with these types was to sit them down (preferably not too close to a tree). For the most part, however, according to Alex, an ounce of prevention could forestall the need to punish at all, like an early verbal warning ("You need to cool it"). Other times those warnings fell on deaf ears, especially when directed toward a female offender transfixed by the whiteness of the lifeguard's teeth when set off by his striking tan. Paul remembers blowing his whistle repeatedly at a group of young women who were pushing each other into the pool, until finally he left his chair to talk to one: "When my lecture was finished her only response was, 'What kind of toothpaste do you use?'"

Paul Aldridge with Swim Pupils

For the truly recalcitrant, the only solution was to throw them out, or even at times to call the police when that person wouldn't leave of his own accord. My brother, Steve, recalls such a case:

"Once there was a truculent patron who didn't think he had to leave when they told him to. I don't know why they were kicking him out, but I remember the police standing there, and Arredondo there in his red bathing trunks with a stance sort of like Yul Brenner, defiantly unafraid of this guy. And Alex wasn't very big,

148

and here he was facing this big guy. Of course, he had the cops backing him up, and the cops took the guy out. I remember Alex saying, 'This guy thinks we can't throw him out, and we need to make sure he understands that we can.'"

I wonder if Alex realized the double lesson that he taught that day, one to an insolent swimmer at the pool, the other—unintended—to a boy in the background, noting his courage and resolve, or if any lifeguard understood how fluid were the designations "watching" and "being watched." From the high-board ladder to the shallow waters of the pool's east end, we too watched them.

In my interviews, for the first time I watched the lifeguards watch themselves, eyes cast back some fifty, sixty, even sixty-five years to access, after all that time, some haunting nugget from their past. It might be the image of one's younger self, of the body in its prime. As Joe puts it, "We were macho. We were lean and mean." Or a snapshot of the moment one embarks on a career, like Alex's recall of his first-day jitters, preparing the pool for its opening day: "My very first day at work there had been a gigantic dust storm the night before, and there was dirt all over the place. Joe came out and said, 'You gotta hurry; you got people waiting, and you're not finished yet.' I thought, 'I'm not going to make it. I'm going to get fired my first day on the job.'" Or, even more consequential, Paul's recollection of finding love at Tempe Beach: "One day I had disciplined her sisters, and Janet came up and apologized for them.... Our first real date was at Monti's. I found an excuse to walk her through the bathhouse first to show her off." Theirs was one of many marriages with courtships set at Tempe Beach. Millie met her husband there. ("When we got married the lifeguards gave us presents.") Today her spouse and Joe Spracale still laugh about the time Joe threw him out.

It is easy to see why, even now, Chuck dreams about "this wonderful time." He is not alone. The lifeguards reigned over a magical place at the very onset of their adult lives and would carry with them, henceforth, much more than remembrance. Chuck discovered the guarding impulse had taken root, had become another reflex, like knee-jerks or blinking: "I was sitting in the Valley Art, and this kid went running down the aisle and I [reaches for the spot on his chest where at Tempe Beach his whistle would have hung]. I didn't have one. But it was instinct: blow the whistle; stop that kid from running." At the pool Joe found not only his niche but his calling in life: "I knew I wanted to be around kids," as did most of the lifeguards, who ended up teaching.

Not surprisingly both Joe and Paul felt the impulse to symbolize, to find in concrete form the very essence of this place (as I, in fantasy, imagine having done—carting off that high-board ladder). Joe, in reality, salvaged from the site a single bench, one of twenty-five or thirty that had been there beneath the trees. A perfect emblem of community, it sits in the History Museum today. When they moved away from Tempe, Paul and Janet too carried with them a keepsake: a river rock from the park that had been, perhaps, a part of the old fence, or—better yet—a part of the bathhouse they had walked through on that first date, headed for Monti's just across the street.

Postcard of La Casa Vieja

Fourth-Day Water

Memoir

When the school year ended in 1963, Daf and I once again set out to hone our skills, not on the diving boards of Tempe Beach, but on the dusty rise behind McKemy Junior High where we would graduate in high heels a few days hence. Up and down the hill we wobbled, veterans of the three-meter springboard, but challenged by the two-inch uplift underneath our heels. That we were here at all attested to our training at Tempe Beach. Practice and pain, inextricably mixed, could lead to success, we had been taught (especially with the competition otherwise engaged). No other girls had thought to rehearse thus, on-site; no others joined us to grapple with this symbol of our passage out of girlhood, this shoe that hobbled and pinched and confined. In a few short days we would stash these heels and return to our bare feet, our bikes, and our two true elements: water and air. The shoes would lie in our closets untouched until the first formal dance of our freshman year at Tempe High. By then Tempe Beach would be but a memory, a fact that, thankfully, we didn't know yet.

In the meantime we picked up where we left off: with our ten-dive repertoires, our scheduled competitions, our exhibitions and, this year, our role as instructors for the children enrolled in "Learn to Dive." This summer I found myself in the strange position of defending a title that I hadn't really won, of being, at least on paper, the defending AAU Senior Open one-meter Champion. In truth I remained the unchallenged challenger, a testament to the adage that half the battle is showing up.

And show up we did, at eight o'clock every morning, plunging into frigid water, attempting dives that terrified us, dodging the swimmers underneath the diving board, arching our backs and pointing our toes, aspiring to a standard we could hardly achieve but caught up in a quest nonetheless, along with the swim team, grueling along to the constant whistle of Marvin, the coach who never got wet, but paced and tweeted as the swimmers ate up laps beside him, and we spun in the air above their heads.

Early in the summer we added instruction to our duties as the yearly Learn to Swim and, more recently, Learn to Dive, programs began. In June of 1962 the pool would boast that one thousand people had participated in its programs since it had opened that year. Of those the most popular by far was Learn to Swim (501) with the newly instituted 50 Mile Swim Club ranking second (185). The other newbie, Learn to Dive, with 150 participants, must have been third. The paper cites John Hollis, lifeguard, as the program's first instructor with Margaret Windsor assisting. But in the program's second year Daf and I filled in, our competence on the boards, it seems, implying a gift for passing that achievement on. But neither of us had a clue. We had learned to dive on our own years before through some combination of pluck and luck. Now trusting mothers handed off their kids to us, two fourteen year olds who were playing it by ear.

I remember how young those children were, little towheads, lining up along the pool's edge, bent with arms extended overhead, while Daf and I tipped them in, flicking their feet up at the end to approximate a vertical, then praising the dive as Chuck praised ours. When this got old one of us—I don't remember which—suggested moving on to the back flip. We lined up the children by the diving boards on that high wall built for swimmers' sprints, then laid out the sequence of a foolproof somersault, a method that might have worked had we factored in the nearness of the wall. Because we hadn't, a head met concrete. I remember comforting the crying child while Daf ran to the bathhouse for ice.

You'd think that after encountering that glitch we would have regrouped, moved on to the forward flip or, better yet, perfected the basic dive we had begun with from this higher platform. Instead we soldiered on, as another head cracked against the wall and another child dissolved in tears. My only explanation for this shocking lack of judgment on the part of Daf and me is how closely equated in our minds were diving and pain. I remember hitting my head on the low board while trying a back flip when I was eleven, then surfacing to see the lifeguard lifted from his chair, poised to dive in had I been really hurt. I remember every dive, at first, producing pain, until one worked out the kinks. What I don't understand is why no one stopped us, why mothers didn't swoop in and rescue their children. I remember only the tears and even some fifty years later the name of the snack bar worker whom Daf called out to: "More ice! Herschel, more ice!!"

Shortly, that voice became just another memory of Tempe Beach. Daf came down with impetigo that summer, a highly contagious skin infection that spread out on her face and chest. The doctors advised that she steer clear of this fill-and-drain pool, whose fourth and fifth days posed a challenge even to healthy eyes and skin. From that point on I remember riding alone with Chuck, or with fellow diver Keith Sipes, to the Valley meets and even once to an on-site scouting of the next day's competition. Chuck came by early and drove me to some pool where I sat in a chair beside the diving tank and watched each competitor perform ten dives, two from each category (forward, backward, inward, reverse, and twist) while baking in the morning sun. When the contest was over, I stood up to leave, wobbling (as I had in my graduation shoes) to the steps, then gripping the rail as I descended to the grass and passed out cold by the poolside. I remember waking in a haze with ants crawling over my arms. Why no one had come to my rescue was clear: dotting the grass all along the pool lay dozens of swimmers, resting from their races. I looked like just another of these. I remember seeing Keith in his green diver's suit within shouting distance of where I lay, but when I tried to summon him I couldn't make a sound. Eventually I recovered, and Chuck drove me back to Tempe Beach where I called my mother, who dutifully left work to drive me home, suggesting that next time I remember breakfast.

The actual meets that year without Daf I can barely recall. The newspaper claims I successfully defended another championship in July ("Sally Cole Takes State 3 Meter Springboard Title") at the Senior AAU meet at Encanto pool. Whether I beat anyone other than my new, younger teammate I can only guess. But it's a safe bet the Dick Smith divers were away again.

The challenge of memoir lies in creating a picture of the long-remembered, and in the process potentially remembering wrong: Was it really Keith Sipes that I saw that day? How many children hit their heads while learning back flips at Tempe Beach? Did Marvin ever get wet? Was the snack-bar worker really named Herschel? Daf doesn't remember teaching those lessons at all, and no one knows for certain who sullied the waters one day with something quite different from the usual band-aids, bobby pins and dibble-dabble sticks: with alligators.

I don't remember who spotted them first, but it was early, before the pool had opened. I was there for diving practice when someone called out from the baby pool. I ran over to find there three baby alligators, quite at home in their enclosure despite the chlorinated water. I remember the photographer arriving from the Tempe Daily News, the hubbub, and then the resumption of practice when it all died down.

Today it is still a mystery who snuck into the pool after hours, deposited the gators, then beat a quick retreat. But as I read the history of Tempe Beach I realize the tradition of scaling the pool fence after hours is as old as that of giving lessons in the mornings. As a child in the forties, Marvin Williams used to do this "quite often... skinny dip, yeah." Even girls got into the act. As Marvin tells it, "My sister and friends used to come down there around 9:30 at night. The cops would come by, they'd run and hide."

At some point the thrill of transgression must have moved beyond bodies to other taboos—those alligators and one night that icon of an earlier time: the cigarette machine that stood outside the snack bar. It must have been a struggle to haul that machine across the cement, through the fence and then into the deep end, and an ever bigger headache to pull it out. I can only imagine the wet tobacco turning the waters a cedar tinge, the mirror catching the sun and throwing it back into our eyes, and I only half-remember swimming around under water and seeing myself in that mirror, my hair floating up mermaid-like, air bubbling out of my nose. That I remember at all is a function of a conversation with my brother, Steve. It went something like this:

Steve: "How about the time someone threw the cigarette machine into the deep end?

Me: "Gee, I don't remember that."

Steve: "You don't? You're the one who told me about it. You called up from diving practice and said you could swim around under water and look at yourself in the mirror, so I got down there as fast as I could before they pulled it out."

Still, Steve himself says he doesn't remember actually taking that plunge or seeing himself underwater in the mirror. I'm not completely certain I do either. The mind selects and modifies its memories, sometimes constructing what it seeks to recall.

Thankfully a newspaper article corroborates my memory of a shocking event at the pool that year: the shooting of lifeguard, Allen Adams. I wasn't there when it happened, but I remember seeing him the very next day, back at the pool with a wound on his arm. The paper describes that wound as superficial. It occurred on June 22nd, about forty-five minutes after "the ejection of two youths, 13 or 14," by Allen, who had the .22 slug removed at Tempe Community Hospital.

I remember the lifeguards fearing a certain sentry post that day, the high chair next to the diving boards where, his face toward Mill, his back to the park, and his shoulders extending from the chair's narrow back, Allen had provided a target for those teens. I can still see Chuck, collapsing his shoulders in, accordion style, to imitate the way he now sat in that chair. But the story ends there, in my mind, just one day after that violent event. Its newsprint version ends there too. When I scan the paper after June 23rd, the day of the article, I find no mention of the shooters or their punishment, no columns on the city's fear or on its outrage, guns in the hands of unsupervised teens.

Strangely, we all forgot in record time that shooting at the swimming pool. More momentous to us must have been the new injunction by Alex Arredondo in mid-July, that henceforth cut-offs would be banned at the beach. This free-wheeling place lost a little of its soul that day. But we carried on, some of us competing in the season's last meets, some of us lying out sizzling in baby oil, the hardiest of us finishing their last long swims toward that ultimate achievement: a summer's tally of fifty miles.

That August would mark my last, most eventful, season at Tempe Beach, one of dives and swoons, of cracked heads and ulcerated skin, of alligators, bullets and cigarette machines. Fourth-day water. And then it was over. On May 30, 1964, a new pool opened at the

Tempe Beach site, our happy swimming pool, with its variable waters, its high diving board, and some forty years of history destroyed. In its place was built a piddling pool with a filter necessitating bathing caps, that aquatic version of the high-heeled shoe. I went there a few times, then never again. Our bathhouse built with WPA funds was pulled down too in a shocking disrespect for a building that embodied the old town itself—Hayden's Ferry—founded on the river whose very stones comprised this structure and the wall surrounding the heralded pool, that "brilliant star in Tempe's crown." The new bath house, with its saddle-shaped roof, would call up images from TV sitcom: the up-swept headgear of The Flying Nun. The new pool's manager, our coach Chuck, must have felt somewhat diminished there, without a high board for his signature dive or a high-dive team to coach at all.

We all moved on to other sites for water play: the valley lakes, canals, and irrigation pumps where we spent the summers of our high school years. We missed out on the chance to dance to the jukebox box in bathing suits, to lie on our towels with the opposite sex, or to fall in love there as generations before us had: we never dated, courted, or even kissed at Tempe Beach.

History

1953-1963
The Fourth Decade of Tempe Beach

Tempe Beach with Slide Pool

It is strange to think of this final decade as a chapter in the history of Tempe Beach, so present does it seem to us, now fifty years older than we were on the night someone drained the pool for the very last time. I wonder which lifeguard opened that drain and whether he knew he would be the last. I wonder if the figeater beetles showed up as the last coins were gleaned from the bottom of the pool, and how many towels were left unclaimed on the fence or on the bathhouse floor. I wonder which song was the last to play on the jukebox by the snack bar stand.

This decade began with the park attracting as many people as the pool itself and ended with picnics a thing of the past. In the early fifties Daf remembers sometimes five or six families eating together on the picnic tables. Afterwards the kids would swim while the parents socialized in the park. The slide pool had been

163

added by then to utilize the space that remained when the pool was shortened to fifty yards, the AAU regulation length. Parents could pack up their picnic gear and watch in their street clothes from behind the fence as their children slid into that new pool. Dan Arredondo remembers his parents, who didn't swim, coming down to the picnic grounds as well: "[Tempe Beach] was like a little family…..My parents would barbecue steaks down there. My buddies and I would go down and eat with them."

Birthday parties and end-of-season swim team bashes were held there too. Alan Holly recalls those celebrations, where swimmers would compete in games, then be recognized for their feats that year: "When the season was over, we'd buy bunches of watermelons, throw them in the pool, and they'd be bobbing up. We'd have all kinds of games, and our families would be there when we got our awards." In the mid-to-late fifties even three-round boxing bouts were held at the park. Danny Frank, Leonard Monti, Jr., and Chuck Lee (a Golden Gloves boxer) remember the ring being set up in the old roller rink first built at the Beach by the WPA.

Tempe High graduation parties revolved around both pool and park, in a fitting testament to their role in promoting students' social growth. According to Harry Mitchell, a typical commencement night might line-up thus: a dance in the gym, a cook-out in Tempe Beach Park, a movie at the College Theater, an all-night swim in the pool, then breakfast at Harman's Big Red Barn. Further evidence that Tempe Beach played a major role in one's high school days is the quiz that was taken by the Class of '61 at their fifty-year reunion in 2011. Having made it to this page, some readers might outscore alums:

1. What was the first name of the grounds keeper inside the pool area?

2. What unwanted animals were found in the "baby pool" circa 1963?

3. How many gallons of water did the pool hold?

4. How many people drowned in the Tempe Beach pool?

5. In what year did the City of Tempe take out the pool and build another smaller pool?

6. Who was the manager of the new, smaller Tempe Beach pool?

7. What did the lifeguards do with coins they found in the pool?

8. Who was Vic Palmer?

9. Did you ever roller skate, box, or play baseball at Tempe Beach?

10. Did you learn to swim, learn to spring-board dive, or take life-saving classes at TB?

11. Name as many TB lifeguards as you can.

12. Which TB dressing room (men's or women's) was typically dirtier at the end of the day?

Birthday, swim-team, and graduation parties were not the only social events at the pool. In the early fifties Tempe Beach was a veritable Match.com, with "most courting and socializing" happening there. In fact, Harry Mitchell recalls many marriage proposals being not just delivered but accepted at the Beach. Alan Holly confirms this view: "My mom met my step-father there, you know. More loves were kindled at the pool than any other place in town." This culture of love must have carried over to the new, smaller pool where both manager Chuck and swimmer Tom Ditsworth first met their wives.

Harry Mitchell is astute in explaining how nostalgia for a swimming pool could run so deep, how an absence could remain present all this time: "The park played a major role in many of the ritual events of town," marking many of its residents' beginnings and ends. Missing is only a birth at Tempe Beach (excluding Marvin's frogs' eggs) or a death (apart from Thornberg's in 1945). In remembering a deceased friend one might, however, find his memory entwined with one's memories of Tempe Beach. When Mark (Dulski) Bryson thinks of his band mate, for example—Harold Aceves, The Hearsemen's/Hobbit's drummer, who died in 2012—he sees him jumping the swimming pool's fence, head wrapped in his towel, and announcing his arrival thus: "I'm Harold of Arabia!"

Original Hobbit 45

Other Voices

Bullets Over Tempe Beach
"You know, you guys, I've been shot."

By all accounts, Allen Adams was calm after being shot that afternoon while guarding from the west-side chair. Everyone remembers his slow descent from that perch beside the high-dive, blood seeping out beneath the hand that grasped his upper arm. It was a massive arm. "Skip" Adams was six foot four and powerfully built. If anyone was born to stop a bullet, it was he.

His calm that day is the point on which all witnesses agree. John Wood, then twelve years old, told my brother Tom he was looking at the lifeguard when a hole appeared in Allen's arm, upon which he merely grimaced, then climbed down from his chair. Alex, then the manager, remembers too this nonchalance: "Allen was so calm. I don't think anyone realized it was a serious situation." John Hollis, who was guarding in the shallow end, saw Allen walking toward him: "He had his hand over his arm and there was blood coming out. I said, 'What in the heck happened to you?' and he said 'I've been shot' and went into the bathhouse." There, Millie Loughrige looked up to hear him remark, "'You know, you guys, I've been shot.' I would have thought, my God, anybody would panic." So unruffled, in fact, was Allen that the bathhouse staff didn't believe him at first.

It would have, indeed, been hard to imagine a shooting at the swimming pool, a place so safe that parents dropped their children off—many still in grade school—day after day without a second thought. That day, June 22nd, was an ordinary afternoon. No one remembers hearing a gun shot, but then who could have with the jukebox blaring, the children screaming and the lifeguards blowing their whistles? And then, out of nowhere, depending on the witness, Allen held up two fingers or blew three short blasts to signal his distress. Alex remembers the former:

"The safety policy I had at the time was you had to stay in your chair. If you wanted anything you had to hold up two fingers. And Allen didn't know he was shot. So he holds up two fingers, and the whistles blow." John Hollis has a different account:

"The pool was a big old long pool, and there were times that we would have so many people in the pool that we'd have to have six lifeguards, but when it was quiet, as it was this afternoon, we would only have two lifeguards, one in the shallow end and then the other one was down in the chair at the deep end. And I was down in the shallow end. We had a signal: if you were going to go in the water and had some kind of emergency, you'd do three real quick blasts on your whistle and then you'd do what you needed to do. So I heard these three blasts from the chair down by the diving boards."

Chuck Holly was there that day too, perhaps in the bathhouse. His cinematic version revolves around a chase scene, five years before we will expect one in our action films, thanks to Steve McQueen in the aptly titled "Bullitt":

"What I remember about it is, I think it was Alex. We thought we'd chase out through that back parking lot and see if we could find the guy that did it. And when we got into the riverbed—remember that river bed was beautiful sand, big salt cedar trees. It was spooky. We looked at each other and it was like, 'He's got a gun. What are we doing?' And we came back."

At some point the wounded "Skip" must have swung past the snack bar where Chuck's brother Alan was working. Having seen him coming, Alan had in mind a friendly prank: "I was ready to grab some ice and throw it at his back, except that I noticed he was grasping his arm, and I noticed blood dripping from the back." Instead of launching his missiles, Alan asked what had happened to be told, "'I got shot,'" and as soon as he said that our heads went down. There were windows on both sides of the snack bar."

Not surprisingly, Alan assumed a shooter with intent—one gunning for Skip—as did the police in suspecting the teens he'd thrown out of the pool just an hour before. If it seems farfetched that two boys would go home, then return with a weapon, Tom Cole puts this theory into context by recalling the culture of early Tempe:

"We all had .22s in those days. I've still got ours, our .22, which is something that every kid—ten years old—had, a .22 rifle. And ours had single shot, bolt action, but the other kids, they had the one with the tube going outside. Just fill it up with all these bullets, and pop-pop-pop-pop-pop-pop. Everyone had one. It's a miracle we didn't shoot each other by mistake, because we were only young kids."

The shooter would have fired, perhaps, according to Alex, from "that grove of trees" in the park behind the pool, or from the riverbed. Alan recalls a policeman who arrived at the pool suggesting that the shot had come from the railroad tracks and was part of a serial shooter's vendetta: "When the police came they said there was a guy going up and down the west coast shooting lifeguards." To complicate these theories, my brother Tom found a bullet shell that very day on First Street by the swimming pool:

"I was there at Mill and Casa Vieja. I looked in the street and there was a .22 bullet shell. I picked it up and rushed home. And I said, "Look at this. I found a bullet shell. Maybe the police would be interested.' Mom said, 'Well, you call them up.' So I called the police up myself. And I said, 'Would you be interested in a .22 bullet shell I found near Tempe Beach?' They said, 'Yes we would.' A few minutes later a policeman arrived at the door. ..and he put out his hand and I put it in there. It was kind of beat-up from being in the street. And he said, 'We'll examine it and see if it matches up to the slug.'"

Unfortunately, no report exists to confirm that match. The Tempe Police Department Records Division located a case number, but not the actual write-up of the case. And, as Alex noted, "They didn't quite have a ballistic means back then," so Tom's find might have been of little use.

In the end, neither the source of that bullet nor the motive for its firing was ever established. Other theories—besides the vengeance of two teenage boys—were posited, among them the chance that Allen, the nephew of the police captain, might have been a stand-in for his Uncle Frank: "It could've been somebody trying to get at the chief, some real criminal trying to mess up his life." Or a jealous lover, as Millie jokes: "Of course the first thing was, 'Have you been messing with anybody's girlfriend or something like that?' And he said, 'No.'" Alex remembers this suggestion too: "There were all kinds of rumors. Allen was a good-looking guy. The other story was...well, you'll have to ask him yourself [laughs]."

When I finally found Allen, at the end of a months-long search, he remembered the police very quickly concluding that the bullet had never been meant for him, but instead had been random, one that missed its tin-can target nearby or that, fired at a distance with no mark in mind, found a hapless victim nonetheless, like a shot pumped skyward on New Year's Eve. He remembered too the sensation of its entry, "a sharp pain in my right arm," concluding at first he'd been hit by a rock, then later, in light of the blood, by a piece of glass from a slingshot blast. Finally, it dawned on him that he'd been shot: "I could feel the bullet, a lump just under the skin that had almost come out the other side."

Why he swung by the snack-bar Allen too made clear. Just after being shot, he noticed a kid at the concession stand look up, spin around, then stuff his wallet into his pants. "I thought it was him," Allen told me, so he climbed down from the chair, pinned the kid against the wall, and pulled the wallet out of his pants. Not surprisingly, as Allen admitted, "I scared him to death!" But since the kid had no weapon, Allen let him go, heading off instead to Tempe Clinic where the staff removed the bullet, one fired from a .22 that, according to the police, should have made a bigger hole.

Today, we all have Allen ("Skip") to thank for his body in the chair that day, its bulk intercepting what might otherwise have felled a child or John (guarding in the shallow end) or Millie (taking a break from the microphone) or Alex or Chuck or Alan (mid-prank) or some luckless driver on the west side of the bridge (ogling the girls in the pool down below), unaware of the bullet hurtling his way as he headed toward Tempe.

Alligators in the Baby Pool
"Boy, that really looks like a real one."

If you Google "Alligators/Tempe Beach" as I did in my earliest musings about this book, you will bring up not the invasion of June 28th, 1963, but a much later incident: "Alligator Brought in to Help Clean up Tempe Town Lake" (July 23, 2010). This alligator—named "Tuesday," after the day the dam had failed—was there to feed on the dying fish produced by that break. The article will document the town's excitement: "My husband texted me from work and said 'You've got to go see the alligator.'" It will make no mention, however, of that parallel event when the same reptile (though multiple and smaller) had ended up at the proximate place, the baby pool of Tempe Beach. If you've ever taught a literature class, you will revisit the sensation of standing before a whole class that has missed the allusion. Even worse you will have the sinking feeling that many readers (and probably the writer herself) are unaware that there once was a swimming pool at Tempe Beach Park.

Those of us who were at the pool that morning—the swim and dive teams and their coaches—will remember that day for years to come, though the details will fade. I remember three, not the four alligators the paper cites in its caption, beneath the picture of Marv and a Tempe policeman named Bill Stevenson standing by the baby pool where "four baby alligators were taken from the waters." I will also forget the younger sibling at the pool that morning who discovered the gators. As Chuck recalls:

"It's 8:30 in the morning. And somebody's little brother came along. He must have been about a six-year-old, so he wasn't on the swim team. But he was playing around in the baby pool; he came up and he's yelling, 'There's alligators in the baby pool.' I mean, I can just remember this kid trying to convince me. Anyway, we finally decided we'd walk down and see what the kid's talking about. Palm fronds? You know, those pieces that fall off? They were alligators."

Little did we know that by this time the police had already been called. Millie Loughrige, the Synchronized Swim coach, had arrived before us, to be met by grounds man Phil Acosta, who headed her off: "He came running up to me, 'Missy, Missy, no, no, no!' And then he showed me: There were alligators in the baby pool." It was Millie herself who called the police with a dime Acosta loaned her. "The Tempe police, they thought it was a joke. They started laughing; they said, 'Oh, sure, lady. I'll send down my alligator squad right away!' Her voice, however, was panicky enough so that the police dispatched an officer: "And by then some of our lifeguards were showing up."

It is surprising that the police would hesitate at all, with the recent spate of gator pranks. As the *Tempe Daily News* explains: "Alligator roundups have become quite common in the past few months." The article goes on to disclose both the origin and fate of these animals: "[They are] part of a haul made several months ago at an abandoned alligator farm east of Mesa. Their relatives and friends were sold in May at the bankruptcy sale and are now residing in a similar facility near Denver." The four recovered from the baby pool that morning were taken to the Maytag Zoo, while two others "found in the Tempe area—one in the Old Main fishpond at ASU and another in a North Tempe canal by youngsters—now are part of the zoo's alligator exhibit." The lake-cleaning "Tuesday" might have been their descendant.

It was my brother Steve who put me on to the story of that alligator farm, a tale he had known for years through his colleague David Lomeli. According to David:

"The story was that Jack Adams himself, the owner of the ranch, just disappeared...and eventually the staff left because they weren't getting paid, so the whole farm was locked down and abandoned. So the alligators were there; they were thriving to some degree, and we as kids then, particularly after learning that the facility was pretty much abandoned, we would jump the fence and play with the alligators. We would throw grapefruit and anything else we could find, particularly at the large alligators, and they would bite the grapefruit and the juice would squirt all over the place."

David McDowell, who worked there at the time, provides a detailed picture of the closing of that farm in 1962. It was run then by a blind man named Dale who told David one morning "to load all of the animals except the alligators in a semi truck owned by a guy named Fritz Whitlock who had a pony ring set up in front of the building":

"I learned that Dale was closing the place and taking everything he could to Missouri. One of the animals was a 650 pound Bengal tiger, which had to be put in a small crate and then transferred into a larger wooden crate in the semi. Getting the tiger loaded was a nightmare but we finally got it done and late that night they left....Fritz called me a few days after they left town and told me that the tiger clawed through the crate and was loose in the back of the semi by the time they reached Lordsburg, N. M. The tiger injured several ponies and had to be shot."

It seems to have been David who first removed an alligator from the farm. In his case, this was not a prank but a method of coping with a boss who had abandoned him as well as the animals. "I was owed two weeks back pay when Dale left, so I took several small alligators and was trying to sell them to people at school." Of course, word quickly spread around Mesa High that the farm was abandoned. Soon other students were making their hauls and freeing small alligators in the irrigation waters on the campus lawn. To this day Mesa High alums are proud of their history of gator dispersal. On their website, mesahighclassof63.com, you can click on "Alligator Tales," and be treated to a photo of the Jack Adams Alligator Farm as well as one of ten Mesa classmates holding three small alligators outside the school.

David Lomeli remembers his brother, Bobby (now deceased) and his friend named Johnny depositing gators around town too, in lakes, canals, and swimming pools; then they'd "wait to hear the headlines, wait to hear the reactions from those who found the gators." One reaction they could not have predicted— when a policeman nearly caught them in the midst of one dispersal trip:

"The cop that pulled them over asked them to open the trunk, and they did in fact open the trunk. And right there in the trunk was a live alligator about three to four feet in length. Now alligators at times will remain completely frozen and to the point where they could actually pass as an artificial alligator or sculpture or some sort of a copy. And the officer looked at the alligator, and the alligator did not flinch. His comment was, 'Boy that really looks like a real one.' And Johnny said, 'Yeah, it does, doesn't it?' So then the cop allowed them to go."

It was not just high schoolers who set loose alligators in the town. It was frat boys too. Chuck learned of this in an unlikely place, a camp ground in Pagosa Springs where his ASU tee shirt attracted the notice of a fellow alum who launched into a gator tale: "And he told me the story. He and some of his fraternity brothers had stolen the alligators, and he didn't say that he put them in the Tempe Beach pool; he said they put them in canals, lakes, things like that. And so when I'm kayaking down the rivers and out on the lakes here, I'm always wondering if there are going to be some alligators."

No one as yet has laid claim to leaving the gators at Tempe Beach, perhaps because that very night the cigarette machine was thrown into the deep end and the snack bar vandalized. In fact, the police even posited a link between the events of this night and the shooting of Allen only three days before. It is easy to see why a person who might otherwise own up to a prank, especially one enacted some fifty years earlier, would be fearful that in this case he might be accused of a real crime.

We will probably never know who put those alligators in the baby pool. And it doesn't really matter. To me, they seem a fitting emblem of the ethnic angst at Tempe Beach—its last bugaboos in the water that, when scooped up and posed before the newsman's camera, revealed themselves for what they were: just babies, and not very scary after all.

Fifth-Day Water

Memoir

After the scouring of Tempe Beach, we sought out water at other sites, water that was cold and clean, or murky—its depths concealed—or moving in an easy flow: urban waters, backwaters, water impoundments, anywhere we could plunge in with hair unbound wearing cutoffs over bathing suits and sneakers on our feet. Anywhere that was not the newly shrunk and filtered Tempe Beach.

A short drive to Baseline would find us at The Pumps, those concrete catch-alls with a massive pipe bearing icy irrigation for the fields that fanned out all around. Except for its angle, perpendicular to the ground, it might have been the pipe that pumped out first-day water with such force that a conditioned swimmer, stroking into it with all his might, would remain in place. Just a year ago I might have been there too, at diving practice on a morning when the pool was not quite filled. Instead, armed with shampoo and razors, conditioner and body cream, we girls now, mid-afternoon, headed out to The Pumps at the margins of town. We had dates that night, and this place was our spa—a kind of hick precursor to a Miraval, or Canyon Ranch.

We'd climb into the hip-high water, then duck under the torrent spewing out of the pipe. That icy output would slam us to the bottom and hold us there with a roaring in our ears. When we needed air, we'd use our feet to push ourselves beyond its bounds, resurfacing to wash our hair, then return for the consummate power rinse. It was more than sensation that we sought. It was the stick-straight hair of Cher and Mary Travers and those California girls we all wanted to be. No kink or wave stood a chance against that pump; then the desert air enforced what the water had decreed as we sat on the low walls shaving our legs.

Joanie had the ultimate in sixties hair; it made a beeline past her shoulders without a single lock off track. What's more, it was blonde. It would reel in boys when we trolled for them on Sunday nights in the downstairs dance hall called JD's. One night, up the road from that club, we stopped at Bob's Big Boy for strawberry pie. A waitress passing by our table spilled a chocolate milkshake on Joanie's head. I can still see her crowned with that dollop of ice-cream complete with whipped cream and a cherry on top, can still remember marveling that of all the spots where it might have landed—on the bald or the graying, on the mousy or the crimped—it instead came to rest on that beach-girl head.

One day at The Pumps Joanie rode on an inner tube under the pipe and was pinned, predictably, beneath its spray. But this time when she needed air she couldn't escape the torrent's hold. After struggling for awhile she experienced that restful letting-go—the hallmark of a drowning death—at which point the pump spewed her free of its sway, and Joanie lived to tell her tale. Not long after this, the city got wind of our escapades and made The Pumps off-limits. But we had other options, post-Tempe Beach.

There was always the Verde. Getting there was a feat in itself, involving dual cars, one left downstream, the other by necessity stuffed to capacity with inner tubes, ice-chests and the whole floating party en route upstream. There, unbound, we'd launch ourselves onto the river, separate but still a unit in our aimless, oddly purposeful, movement toward that downstream car. Occasionally, we'd have to paddle to break free of some sluggish pool. Mostly, we just drifted. We were "chill" before there was a word to name it, that lazy state on the border between motion and stasis. We moved without moving, the river lulling us while carrying us along.

Once, during college, Wendy brought two classmates home, wealthy prep-school boys, one from Princeton, the other from Shaker Heights. She knew a river trip would wow even them, and the whole clan set out for a day in the sun. The boys quickly found a source of amusement, enlivening the otherwise Zen-like float. Paddling well ahead of us, they'd call back, in urgent tones, their volume on high: "WATCH OUT! JUST AHEAD THERE'S A HUGE DNCUO BRINDSTZO WAH," the kernel of their warning completely obscured. When we'd shout back a frantic "WHAT?" or "WHERE?" they'd return a new gibberish stream: "A REALLY BIG AND DANGEROUS CRISKEN DOYZ PRIBOTX!!" Even when we'd caught on, they kept it up, clearly enamored of their wit until, spotting the place where we'd dropped off that initial car, they paddled toward shore.

The float had ended, but not the hilarity. In a minute or two I drifted by, so thoroughly chill from the lapping waters and their rocking sway that I sat up, startled, and said to them, "Hey! This isn't where we got in." The hoots of laughter were not the only reason I recall this day. My father, in addition to laughing, fashioned a label for his second child, one I struggle with to this day: "You're the dumbest smart girl I ever met!" My memories of the Verde are thus overlaid with shame. It is small consolation that my father's pronouncement could have been much worse: "You're the smartest dumb girl I've ever met."

More often, on the river, I was with my peers. In our lust for adventure, we'd be drawn, mid-float, to a towering rock along the shore. Here stood a natural replacement for the high dive at Tempe Beach. While low enough to beckon, it was high enough to challenge; few people feared it enough to pass when we beached ourselves and made our climb. I must have jumped there dozens of times. But when I try to envision it, to picture my teen companions plunging from that rock, I see only cut-offs, bikini tops, and cheap Keds sneakers in their circuit from that brink, through the air into the river, and then back again. The faces are a blur.

What I do see instead is the day, years later, when I paused there on a float-trip with my husband and a friend who'd come in from LA. I had left my baby, just eight months old, with my mother in Tempe. I scrambled happily up the rock to take what, I assumed, would be the first of several leaps. To my shock, I couldn't do it and instead climbed down. I wasn't afraid. But a baby impinged on my freedom that day. Somewhere on the road from the Pink Shadow Club to competitive diving, from college to seedy apartments, to grad school and marriage and then late-night childbirth at Desert Sam—in increments so miniscule they hadn't even registered—I must have grown up.

Or maybe I was just remembering that other cliff at Canyon Lake. It was high, so high—higher than the high-board (above which I'd promised never to go), higher than the tower, higher than the bridge to its right stretching out below. It was forty feet high, at its apex a cable, the source of its name. At some point in a lake trip we'd end up at "The Cable" where the macho swaggered in their sneakers and sweatshirts while bathing beauties watched from their towels in the sun. It was all so familiar—the cushioning clothes, the strut and the bombast—this build-up to a splash-dive-on-steroids from a cliff jutting out into the water, and thus compelling not only courage but a running start.

Because of The Cable, I had more than my share of lake-dates that year, as did a classmate, Cheryl. We won out for our common gift: a power to humiliate and thus provide not only amusement but a short-cut to dominance for those by our sides. First we'd climb up the cliff and lay out our towels within earshot of the bluster and the crowing and the whoops. When these boys had sufficiently established dominion, had marked this turf as their manly own, Cheryl and I (barefoot, bikini-clad) would rise in silence and run off the edge.

Cheryl always screamed as she plummeted. I was quiet, arms wide-flung, until I got my bearings, at which point I'd bring my arms to my sides, close my legs and point my toes, as Chuck had taught me to do. In that position and with such momentum, I'd hit the water like a hot knife through butter, to create what, as I recall, was the scariest part of a Cable jump: that struggle to the surface so far away. My ascent would be hampered by the fact that one hand, instead of assisting

185

in the journey toward air, would be trying to unwrap from around my throat the bikini top that had wound up there.

Given the time it took to surface, reposition bratops, and reclimb the cliff, we always missed out on the drama up top. Our only clue as to what had transpired was an eerie quiet and the full-face grins that our dates both wore. Cheryl and I might jump once more, then leave with the boys who, through some form of transference, had become—without hazarding a single jump—the new Alpha males.

It is hard to smile when remembering these trips, in light of what happened at The Cable one day. A school mate whose locker had been just above mine did a back flip from the cliff, hit the water wrong and died. The police closed off The Cable after that. I remember sitting at the kitchen table with a sibling or two when we'd just found out. My mother walked in, looked at me and said, "I trust YOU never jumped off that cliff." In our house lying was a capital crime. When I didn't answer, she just shook her head and walked away.

Given a childhood steeped in water, it is fitting I would wind up in a swamp. In New Orleans even the air was wet. Rain fell for hours, establishing puddles where tadpoles grew. Sweat pooled. Hair frizzed. When alligators showed up, there had been no prank. Then one day the levees broke, filling the town with a record-setting pre-drain count: twenty-first-day water sitting roof-high in houses, water that, when finally drained, left a bathtub ring around the town.

Barataria Preserve, Louisiana

So I moved back home, or at least close-by—to Tucson, a town whose dishevelment more closely resembled old Tempe. My actual home, that revamped place, scarcely rang a bell, its streets become highways, its bars become brew-pubs, and its old retail corridor completely overhauled. Only the Valley Art (Red Harkins' hybrid theater) and the Casa Vieja brought to mind those long summer journeys—stomachs rumbling, feet on fire—along sidewalks that had been our path all those years ago to Tempe Beach.

History

New Tempe Beach Pool

When the people of Tempe approved a bond issue on October 29, 1963, with turnout setting a new city record, they could not have imagined their "yes" votes would set in motion the all-out destruction of Tempe Beach: the swimming pool, the bath house and the long-established cottonwoods that marked the site. The issue wasn't framed that way. In the days before the actual vote, the paper advanced a less drastic plan, announcing on October 12th that in addition to building a new swimming pool the city would allocate $50,000 for the modernizing of Tempe Beach so that health requirements could be met. On the 18th the vote was defined as a nod to "remodel and update" the pool. On the 23rd it was once again cast as a vote to "modernize" Tempe Beach.

And yet as early as June, the minutes of a Parks and Recreation Special Council Meeting show another option on the table. At that meeting members weighed the "advisability of maintaining Tempe Beach versus arranging for other swimming pool facilities." In July they pointed out, with justification, the signs of wear at the forty-year-old pool:

"The picture at Tempe Beach is not so bright. The water is maintained at a healthful level, but the decking around the pool is cracked and unsafe. Besides this, the bath house continues to present problems because of the antiquated plumbing and electricity. More rough spots are showing up at the bottom of the pool which also adds to the problem."

In August their monthly report cited water issues as the heart of the problem, referencing the one day the pool had to close and the several others where hours were curtailed. I could find no record of the reasoning behind the decision to tear down, not fix up this pool. But less than one month after the bond issue passed, at their meeting of November 23rd, a special Parks and Recreation Board had toured Tempe Beach and seen the blueprints of a Plan A and Plan B drawn up by H. W. Krussman's engineering firm. Present at that meeting were Jean Bryant, Robert Svob, Louis Scherer (Public Works Director), Krussman (consulting engineer), Sam Fees, Max Connolly, Joe Salvato, Dr. Mortensen and Janis Kellogg. The plan to build a new pool must have been in the works for some time by then.

At the next month's meeting of the P & R Board and Council an unnamed "I" makes his case for what was surely the Plan A version of the tear-down: a 25 by 45 foot pool with a depth of three to five feet, a 25 by 45 foot wading pool, a separate diving tank with a thirteen-foot depth and a multi-purpose bath house. For reasons I could neither find nor imagine, it was Plan B that carried the day, its parameters laid out in a front-page sketch on February 7, 1964, in the *Tempe Daily News*. No diving tank has made the cut, and no high board dominates the now-shallow deep end. The old pool's grassy lawn and cottonwood trees have been swapped out for large swaths of pavement in the interest of hygiene. An ultra-modern bath house eclipses the pool, its historic forebear having lost out to this architect's version of a trophy wife.

From my fifty-year vantage point, the article accompanying this sketch has its tone all wrong, flippant and irreverent. Once known as the city's "brilliant star," the old pool is now described as a withered crone: "The old gal's name will remain the same, but she's in for a major face lift in the days ahead, and you won't recognize her when she gets back into operation this spring." One sentence later the face-lift more accurately becomes euthanasia: "Most of the existing facilities will be swept away in a major renovation." Ten firms, the article tells us, have already bid on the project, which came in over budget at $127,200, due largely to the high-end bath house "which was not in the talk of $50,000 to update the pool."

It is hard to find people today who remember the details of this decision. After all, a City- Council or Parks-and-Recreation member who was thirty then would be eighty today. Fortunately, in January 1999 architect Michael Wilson Kelly created a "Document for Posterity on the Swimming Pool Facility at Tempe Beach Park." In it Joe Spracale, Harry Mitchell, Ron Pies, Skip Bryant and Dawne Walczak share their memories of the old Tempe Beach and the pool that replaced it. According to this document, it was Joe Salvato, the Parks and Recreation head, who championed the building of a new, smaller pool. No one I talked to spoke highly of him. And yet many concur with his contention that a small pool would benefit the town. Coach Marv, for example, told me swim teams then were doing a lot of short-course racing—twenty-five meters—and also that the small pool worked well recreationally for younger kids. Harry Mitchell agreed that at that time "twenty-five yards was the new competitive length." In addition, it is hard to dispute the benefits listed in the Document for Posterity:

> "state-of-the-art filtration, drainage and chlorination systems, improved maintenance capability, better access control, improved hygienics, a new spray-fountain baby pool, generous paving for sun bathing, and better surveillance of activities by lifeguards and staff."

Some of us might question whether "generous paving" would count as an improvement over lying on the lawn of the old Tempe Beach, and that last advantage is highly ironic: only two years after the new pool opened a child drowned within yards of the lifeguard stand despite the filtered, never murky water. And yet on the whole, as Ron Pies notes, the Olympic-sized facility was in dire need of updates. Who can imagine the continued practice of draining a pool three times a week?

But the plan had many detractors as well, one objection being a "perceived lack of use." Skip Bryant points out that "the population living closest to Tempe Beach Park was aging, and less inclined to participate in activities there," while the younger families who might use the pool were moving farther east and south. Others were building their own backyard pools. It would be hard, thus, to justify the cost of the new pool. In addition, a small pool would hardly have the "regional draw" that the old pool had had, nor would it be adequate for hosting competitions—the AAU meets, the Junior Olympics—as the old pool had with as many as 800 competitors a year. As Rudy Campbell told me, Tempe Beach would become just a "little city pool," that had "lost its allure" and, worse, "wasn't fun any more."

Nostalgia was the basis for most objections to the new swimming pool. For forty years Tempe Beach had been the "focal point not only to Tempe, but to the entire Valley—socially, culturally, and recreationally." The park, too, had drawn crowds: picnickers, baseball players, skaters, boxers, bowlers, and had done so with few rules— no leash laws, no curfews and no problem with loitering. Most importantly, the report cites the "natural beauty of the setting," as the town's greatest loss: its "openness," its atmosphere of freedom "unparalleled to this day in Tempe." It is no exaggeration to mark as "sacred" what remains of the cobblestone bleachers, ball park and stone wall—even the name "Tempe Beach Park"—as this report does.

In the end, that these detractors were right is small consolation, given all that was lost. What we know today—that historic places should be preserved—was lost on the city leaders then. As Ron Pies puts it: "The climate of the times did not recognize the historic value of the cobblestone structures; rather they were thought of as 'just plain old' and outdated." Irresistible, by contrast, was the Modern International Style of the new bath house with its "thin-shelled concrete hyperbolic paraboloid roofs." You'd think that description alone would have warned them off.

The pool projected to last twenty-five years was closed in only ten, then abandoned for another ten until in 1985, filled with sand, it became a sculpture garden. Today the site is a grand promenade between Mill Avenue and Tempe Town Lake. Michael Kelly's document is harsh in its pronouncement: "The cobblestone historic structures and walls are now sorely missed but the 196[4] pool facility will not be."

I hardly remember the new pool at all, having gone there only a couple of times, put off by the bathing-cap rule. Yet I must have complained to my father at length, given Tom's recollection of two gatherings around the kitchen table at about that time:

"Dad was reading this letter to Bill Wood, saying 'Who was the mastermind?'—so this was his refrain—"Who was the mastermind who decided in the girls' locker room there would be no doors on the dressing stalls?' Didn't like the way it was. The next day they were there again, having a beer at the kitchen table. (As Steve says, the drama of life goes on around Formica tables). And there was Dad. He looked at Bill Wood, and he said, 'You know, Bill, remember that letter I wrote yesterday? Not gonna send it—gave up on it.' So he had slept on it and thought better of actually sending this truculent letter to the *Tempe Daily News.*"

It is strange now to hear my father's words and imagine him—a man who had never swum in the old pool himself or even picnicked in the park—raging at the kitchen table over so small an item, the missing doors on the dressing stalls. I can see now his anger was mine, and those doors but a metaphor for the town's real loss: its Common—a lush green space with benches under cottonwoods and a mammoth pool, its water so cold and clear that today, after fifty years, the shock of it still registers.

Aerial View of the Pool, circa 1940

Acknowledgments

I couldn't have written this book by myself. I needed the help of a whole community, and that community was more than willing to give me its time as well as its stories: in interviews, on the telephone, and in email messages and Facebook threads. Thanks first to the lifeguards—Paul Aldridge, Alex and Dan Arredondo, John Hollis, Chuck Holly, Eldon Smith, Joe Spracale, Don Wilkinson, and Marvin Williams, and to Allen Adams (when I finally found him) who told me the details of the day he was shot. Thanks to Millie Loughrige, the synchronized swim coach, and to all the members of both swim teams: Alan Holly, Elissa Montgomery Tap, Cindy Statz Mattoon, Charlene Mills Ashworth, Tom Ditsworth, Frank Downey (and to Eldon again); Margaret Winsor Maciborka, Mary Jane Wegner Torok, Linda Carnal Whatley, Valerie McMillion and Nancy Leach Lesko, as well as diver Keith Sipes.

I am grateful for the responses to my queries on the site "Remember Tempe, AZ When" by JoAnn Voss Brown, Tom Voss, Mark Dulski Bryson, Donna Wells, Gerry Turley, Jim Settlemoir, Ruth Corson, David Link, Katharine Karyszyn (FKA Deborah Hood), Diane Follette Lisonbee, Fred Stone, Deborah Campbell Austin and Janice Hollis Strickland, and also for the email responses from Doug Royse, Buddy Davis, Doug McQueen, and Mark Bailey. Thanks to Steve Hancock for writing the wonderful essay, "A Trip to Tempe Beach," which everyone should read and to Bill Lee for his help on the history of boxing at Tempe Beach.

My thanks also to the "old settlers" of Tempe—Harry Mitchell, Rudy Campbell, and Peggy Bryant— for their help with my project, to Joe Spracale for sharing his pictures, and to David Lomeli and David McDowell for their alligator tales.

Family and friends, as always, came through for me—Laure Wegner Kagen, Joanie Johnson Hartman, and Daf Livingston Rutz told me stories. In addition, Daf put me in touch with many old Tempeans and with Payson resident Cindy Whatley, all who added to my narrative; Daf also encouraged me, helped me with my interviews and scanned many photos for the book. My old New Orleans friend Catherine Loomis, a wonderful writer, read the manuscript and offered her suggestions.

Thanks to my siblings for their excellent memories—Tom, Steve, Jeff, and Wendy Cole—and also to Wendy for helping me locate several people in this book. In addition, Steve drew the alligator on page 173; Tom contributed his considerable technical skills as well as giving me a place to sleep on my many trips from Tucson to Tempe. My children Chris, Davy, and Kate Mooney—all three writers themselves—offered their suggestions for improving my book.

I want especially to thank the Tempe History Museum for its excellent collection of documents and photographs and curator Jared Smith for providing a space for my interviews and for helping me navigate the research room.

Finally, I can't thank Chuck Holly enough for teaching me to dive all those years ago. That experience, more than anything else, compelled me to write this book.

Preface

iv **On Sundays**: Joe Spracale, Interview with the author, February 2, 2012.

iv **Brilliant star**: Dean Smith, *Tempe—Arizona Crossroads: An Illustrated History (Chatsworth, Calif.*: Windsor Publications, 1990) p.68.

FIRST-DAY WATER

Memoir

6 **Dibble dabble**: For an interesting history of the game see Corey Kilgannon, "All Hail the Dibble Queen, *New York Times*, August 10, 2012. http://www.nytimes.com/2012/08/12/nyregion/lisa-mueller-gannon-reigns-as-the-dibble-queen.html?_r=0

History 1923-1933

9 **July 11, 1923**: J. F. Weeks, "Tempe," *The Arizona Gazette,* July 12, 1923, p. 4. The accepted date for the opening of Tempe Beach seems to be the date that the pool began charging admission. The pool itself had been open to the public before this date.

10 **First person ever**: William Windes, Interviewed by Julie Christine, Oral History Transcript 119, June 10, 1987, Tempe History Museum, p. 16.

10 **What we called vero**: Ray M. Chavarria, Interviewed by Scott Solliday, Oral History Transcript 136, August 17, 1963, p. 29.

10 **Point-in-the-rock, Jointhead**: Windes, OHT, pp. 13-14. Also Michael Curry, Jr., (Edward), interviewed by Julie Christine, Oral History Transcript 105, August 17, 1987, p. 20. These swimming holes are also described in the *Tempe News,* July 14, 1916. Excerpts from these early newspaper articles may be found in the card catalogue of the Tempe History Museum under the heading "Tempe Business Survey Index M-Z."

10 **2-3,000 people**: Edward Curry, Oral History Transcript 105.

10 **Land bought by Charles Hayden**: Patricia Blaine, "Tempe Beach Park: A Joint Project between Tempe Historical Museum and the Public History Program at ASU," December 13, 2002, pp. 8-11. Hayden AZ Collection CM MSM-739, ID # 60558. Luhrs Reading Room, Hayden Library. Also in Gray Matter Files, Tempe History Museum. Blaine gives a detailed account of the land transactions in addition to the money paid. See also *Arizona Republic,* April 27, 1952, for information on the bonds.

10 **4% interest**: R. J. Stroud, "Tempe Beach Pool and Playground," *Tempe News* c. 1937. This useful article has been photo copied, but no date appears. It has been cited as having been

written in 1933 but was obviously written much later, given its discussion of the Far Western Swim Meet at Tempe Beach, held in 1937.

11 **Garfield Goodwin**: *Tempe News*. April 18, 1923. **Stolberg**: *Tempe News,* April 25, 1923. **Fence**: *Tempe News*. April 20, 1923. **Well**: August 8, 1923. For details on the building of the pool, see also AZ State Historical Property Inventory (HPS 190), Tempe History Museum.

11 **Art Clark**: Art Clark, "Tempe Beach Pool Was Center of Fun, Fellowship," *East Valley Tribune*, August 28, 1996: B2.

11 **100,000 swimmers**: *Tempe News*. December 18, 1930. Card catalogue, THM. This excerpt also gives total cash receipts and net profit.

12 **175 by 60 feet**: R. J. Stroud, "The History of Tempe Beach and Playground."

12 **Early patron**: *Tempe News,* April 27, 1929. Excerpt in THM card catalogue.

13 **Everybody met here**: www.youtube.com/watch? v=1cSp9wjGRTg

13 **It was the big place**: Marvin Williams, Interview with the author, February 17, 2012. All subsequent quotes taken from this interview.

13 **Third place**: Ray Oldenburg, *The Great Good Place: Cafes, Coffee Shops, Bookstores, Bars, Hair Salons and Other Hangouts at the Heart of a Community (* DaCapo Press, 1989), p. 41, 32.

14 **Stroud, records could be set there**: Christine Marin. "LULAC and Veterans Organize for Civil Rights in Tempe and Phoenix 1940-1947." MASRC Working Paper #29, p. 3.

14 **1925 AAU meet; 1927 AAU meet**: Sarah Martin, "A Community Center: Tempe Beach and Playground, 1923-1945," A Joint Project between Tempe Historical Museum and the Public History Program at Arizona State University, December 18, 2002, p. 7. This article is in the THM Gray Matter file.

14 **Praise for Dr. Stroud**: "Praise for Dr. Stroud," TB Exhibition Notebook, Scrapbook 1924-1933, referencing the 8th Annual AAU Open Swim Meet, August 25, 1932. It is uncertain where this article appeared, but it was probably in the *Tempe News.*

15 **Holm record**: Martin, p. 9. See also *The Phoenix Gazette,* vol. L11, September 10, 1932. This article has the race results. Holm won the 220 yard backstroke in 2 minutes, 57 8/10 seconds, 2 4/5 seconds faster than the previous mark.

15 **This chaperone came up to me**: www.swimmingworldmagazine.com/lane9/news/6702.asp

16 **Though its tower will be gone**: R. J. Stroud, "The History of Tempe Beach and Playground." In this article, Stroud says that the tower lasted twelve seasons.

16 **Lois Williams**: Marvin Williams interview.

16 **Jose Guaderrama**: "Time Line," Tempe Beach Exhibition Notebook, Tempe History Museum.

Other Voices

Childhood at Tempe Beach

17 **I remember working on**: Jeff Cole email, January 16, 2012.

18 **Going over to the baby pool**: Tom Cole, Interview, January 5, 2012. All subsequent quotes from Tom Cole come from this interview.

18 **Tempe Beach is where I took swimming lessons**: Jim Settlemoir, "Remember Tempe, AZ When," Facebook thread, April 10, 2012.

19 **They threw a bunch of goldfish**: JoAnn (Voss) Brown, "Remember Tempe, AZ, When," Facebook thread, April 10, 2012.

19 **Whatever kids wanted to do**: Alex Arredondo, Interview with the author, February 23, 2010. All subsequent quotes from Alex come from this interview.

20 **We'd be trying to save someone**: Alex Arredondo.

20 **A very relaxed and liberal dress code**: Steve Cole, Interview with the author, January 11, 2012. All subsequent quotes from Steve, unless otherwise indicated, come from this interview.

20 **Once I had a wet sweatshirt**: Mary Jane (Wegner) Torok, Interview with the author, July 17, 2012. All subsequent quotes from Mary Jane come from this interview.

21 **Bubble-bomb**: Jeff Cole, Email, January 18, 2012.

22 **One requirement for our Water Badge**: Laure (Wegner) Kagen, conversation, February, 2012.

22 **What I remember most**: David Link , July 24, 2010. www.tempehighbuffs68.com/forum_topic.php?topicid=75 .

22 **His slow time under water**: Donna Wells, "Remember Tempe, AZ, When," Facebook thread, April 24, 2012.

23 **As a conditioned football lineman**: Gerry Turley, "Remember Tempe, AZ When," Facebook thread, April 26, 2012.

23 **For ridiculous counts**: Jeff Cole, Email, January 18, 2012.

23 **Dick Smith**: William Norris, *Willful Misconduct: The Shocking Story of Pan American Flight 806 and Its Startling Aftermath* (New York: W. W. Norton & Company, 1984), 26. In

this book Dick Smith is referenced by the pseudonym Leon Martin.

23 **One of U of A's swimmers**: Tom Ditsworth, Email, May 11, 2012.

24 **Multiple Dibble Dabble**: Jeff Cole, Email, June 25, 2012.

25 **When the pool was a little murky**: Joanie (Johnson) Hartman, "Remember Tempe, AZ When," Facebook thread.

25 **Tokens of this game**: Linda (Carnal) Whatley, Email, February 9, 2012. All subsequent quotes from Linda come from this email.

26 **The turnstile gate**: Joanie and Steve, "Remember Tempe, AZ When", Facebook thread.

26 **Approximately 200 bikes**: Doug Royse, Email to Daphne (Livingston) Rutz, February 14, 2012.

26 **Grill around the drain**: Charlene (Mills) Ashworth, Email, January 22, 2013. All subsequent quotes from Charlene are taken from this email.

26 **Waterfall feature**: Elissa (Montgomery) Tap, Email, November 10, 2012. All quotes from Elissa come from this email.

26 **Colors**: Tom Ditsworth, Email, May 11, 2012; Doug Royse, Email, February 14, 2012; Steve Hancock, "A Trip to Tempe Beach," www.tempehighbuffs68.com/forum_topic.php?topicid=75

27 **Smells**: Jeff, Email, January 18, 2012.

27 **Jukebox**: Wendy, Email, February 18, 2012; Dan Arredondo, Interview with the author, March 7, 2012 .(All subsequent quotes from Dan come from this interview); Joe Spracale, Interview with the author.

28 **You were right on the end of it**: Chuck Holly, Interview with the author, February 2, 2012. Unless otherwise indicated, all quotes from Chuck are taken from this interview.

28 **The swimming-pool dream**: Chris Dickey, *Summer of Deliverance: A Memoir of Father and Son* (New York: Touchstone, 1998). Quoted in Lisa Miller, "Can Science Explain Heaven," *Time* (March 26, 2010). www.lisaxmiller.com/can-science-explain-heaven/1827

Getting to Tempe Beach

31 **Bare feet**: Jeff, Email, February 29, 2012.

31 **With his dog**: Harry Mitchell, Phone Interview with the author, March 2013.

32 **Barefoot to Tempe Beach**: Nancy (Leach) Lesko, Email, February 9, 2012.

32 **Under the underpass on Mill**: Wendy Cole, Email, February 18, 2012

32 **Jericho the donkey**: Charlene (Mills) Ashworth, Email, January 22, 2013.

32 **Tracks from Daley Park**: Jeff, Email, February 29, 2012.

33 **The white painted lines**: Tom Voss, "Remember Tempe, AZ When," Facebook thread, April 10, 2012.

33 **Those stickers**: Jeff, Email, February 29, 2012.

34 **Bullheads are invincible**: Jim Settlemoir, "Remember Tempe, AZ When," Facebook thread, April 11, 2012.

34 **We all got bused to Daley Park**: Ruth Corson, "Remember Tempe, AZ When," Facebook thread, April 11, 2012.

35 **Brother vanished for a day**: Katharine Karyszyn (FKA Deborah Hood), "Remember Tempe, AZ When," Facebook thread, April 11, 2012.

36 **Warm-up pranks**: Jeff, Email, February 29, 2012.

36 **Miller's Indian Store**: Steve Hancock, "A Trip to Tempe Beach," 5.

37 **Billboard with an ocean scene**: Sharon Southerland (Westwood '66). Email from Doug McQueen, April 4, 2013.

38 **Extra-large safety pin**: Mark Bailey, Email, April 4, 2013.

38 **Penelope du Chantelet**: Millie Loughrige, Interview with the author, July 16, 2012. All subsequent quotes from Millie are taken from this interview.

39 **Coldest water fountain in town**: Mark Bailey, Email, April 4, 2013.

39 **Hitting up his dad**: Buddy Davis, Email to Daphne Rutz, February 7, 2012.

39 **Large plate of french fries**: Doug Royse, Email to Daphne Rutz, February 14, 2012.

40 **Sugar cookie**: Eldon Smith, Interview with the author, July 16, 2012. All subsequent quotes from Eldon are taken from this interview.

40 **Pecan Crispy**: Steve Hancock, "A Trip to Tempe Beach," p. 4.

SECOND-DAY WATER
History 1933-1943

51 **Bathhouse, other improvements**: Sarah Martin, pp. 3-6. See also Appendix.

52 **Red Harkins**: Tempe Beach Exhibition Notebook, 1924-33. Tempe History Museum; See also Stan Schirmacher, "Tempe Beach Theatre," in Historical Property Survey 190, Tempe History Museum. Schirmacher was the doorman at the old State Theatre across the street from Carr Mortuary. He includes many details about the single-season Tempe Beach Theatre, including the opening feature ("Riptide") and the attraction that filled the house ("Viva Villa").

52 **Second feature**: *Five Branded Women*, Directed by Martin Ritt, 1960. On watching this film again in 2013, I was surprised at how tame it seemed.

53 **Baseball field**: Martin, pp. 11-13.

54 **Swim meet program**: Tempe Beach Exhibition Notebook. Tempe History Museum. All quotes taken from this official Far-Western Meet program.

55 **Wright Junior College**: "Synchronized Swimming," Wikipedia. www.en.wikipedia.org/wiki/Synchronized_swimming

55 **Exponent of pulchritude**: "World Champions Arrive to Swell List in Swim Meet," *Phoenix Gazette*, vol. L11, September 6, 1932, p. 1.

55 **Salacious text**:" Big Weekend in Sports," *Phoenix Gazette*, September 10, 1937, p. 6.

56 **150 Medley**: "Records Shattered as Final Program of Meet is Staged," *Arizona Republic*, September 13, 1937, Sec. 2, p. 3.

56 **Disadvantaged by the early start**: R. J. Stroud, "Tempe Beach Park and Playground."

57 **Our coach Millie**: Linda Whatley, Email, February 9, 2012.

No Mexicans Allowed

57 **May 21, 1946**: Although this is the date cited as the day restrictions ended at Tempe Beach, it was actually not until May 22nd that "local Americans of Mexican descent" were allowed in the pool. *Tempe Daily News*, p. 1.

57 **Uniform practice**: Robert B. McKay, "Segregation and Public Recreation," *Virginia Law Review*, vol. 40 no. 6 (October 1954), 701, quoted in www.peoplesguidetomaricopa.blogspot.com/2011/05/tempe-beach-park.html

58 **Antonio Celaya**: Scott W. Solliday, "The Journey to Rio Salado: Hispanic Migrations to Tempe, Arizona," (M. A. thesis, Arizona State University, 1993) 117. A rough draft of this thesis is in the Tempe History Museum.

58 **Anglos/Mexicans in old Tempe**: Blaine, pp. 12-13. See also "Hispanic History," www.tempe.gov/index.aspx?page=1372

58 **Anglos understood Spaniards**: Joseph A. Rodriguez, "Becoming Latinos: Mexican Americans, Chicanos, and the Spanish Myth in the Urban Southwest," *The Western Historical Quarterly,* vol. 29, no. 2 (Summer, 1998) pp. 165-185. Quoted in peoplesguidetomaricopa.blogspot.

58 **Lillie Perez story**: Sarah Martin. A copy of this letter of protest is in the appendix.

59 **Williams Air Force Base story**: Marin, pp. 3-4. See also Jennifer Lambert, "Tempe Beach: A Cultural Resource Study 1942 to Present," ASU History Department, 2002, p. 1. Gray Matter File, THM.

59 **Roosevelt quote**: Marin, p. 3.

59 **Murdock address**: "Week's Doings," *Tempe News*, April 18, 1942, p. 3.

60 **Cole/Connolly response**: Marin, p. 4.

60 **Separate pool**: "500 Fund for Mexicans," *Tempe News*, July 14, 1939. See also Sarah Martin, 13-14 and Christine Marin, p. 5.

61 **Tempe ditch day**: Josie Ortega Sanchez, Interviewed by Richard Nearing, Oral History Transcript 126, June 23, 1992, pp. 17-18. Tempe History Museum.

62 **Garbage truck**: Elizabeth Montanez Rivera, Oral History Transcript excerpt, Tempe Beach Exhibition Notebook, Tempe History Museum.

62 **Miami, AZ pool**: Ray Flores, "Part 3, The Reform," *Arizona History: A Chicano Perspective 1750-1950,"* Tucson, Chicano Media Productions, 1985. This video is available at the Fletcher Library, ASU West Campus.

63 **No malice**: Alex Calderon, Oral History excerpt, Tempe Beach Exhibition File, THM.

63 **Federal judge**: Solliday, p. 117.

63 **Leases**: Sarah Martin, p. 5. Photocopies of these leases appear in the appendix.

64 **Manipulation of leases**: Marin, p. 5.

64 **Martinez**: Ray Martinez, Interview with Jean Reynolds, November 16, 1999. Arizona History Museum.

Other Voices

The High Diving Board

68 **Individuals may uncork**: Oldenburg, p. 58; **stage**: p. 59.

68 **Dumb trick**: Jeff, Email, January 18, 2012.

69 **Canine sketch**: Jeff, Email, January 22, 2012.

70 **Way up there**: Jeff, Email, January 22, 2012.

71 **Bloody nose**: Tom Voss, "Remember Tempe, AZ When," Facebook thread, June 2, 2012.

72 **Sharp crack**: David Link, tempehighbuffs68, July 24, 2010.

72 **Double**: Daf (Livingston) Rutz, conversation, February, 2012.

72 **Malfunction**: Diane (Follette) Lisonbee, "Remember Tempe, AZ, When," Facebook thread, June 3, 2012.

73 **Hit the board**: Keith Sipes, Email, February 9, 2012.

73 **My mouth caught the board**: Charlene (Mills) Ashworth, Email, January 22, 2013.

73 **Right back on the board**: Daf, conversation, February, 2012.

73 **Louganis**: You can watch this dive on you tube: http://www.youtube.com/watch?v=L5nqeFWufrE

74 **Double-dog dare**: JoAnn (Voss) Brown, "Remember Tempe, AZ When," Facebook thread, June 3, 2012.

The Snack Bar

76 **Those taffy sheets**: Susan (Abbott) Holmboe, "Remember Tempe, AZ When," Facebook thread, July 14, 2012.

77 **1908 dime**: Fred Stone, "Remember Tempe, AZ When," Facebook thread, April 24, 2012.

77 **Bean tostados**: Cindy (Statz) Mattoon, Email. All subsequent quotes from Cindy are taken from this email.

78 **Ever eating anything**: Deborah "Campbell" Austin, "Remember Tempe, AZ When," Facebook thread, July 15, 2012.

78 **The meat was marbled**: Alan Holly, Interview with the author, July 17, 2012. All subsequent quotes from Alan are taken from this interview.

80 **Don was an athlete**: John Hollis, Interview with the author, July 16, 2012. All subsequent quotes from John are taken from this interview.

Third-Day Water
Memoir

90 **Plane crash**: William Norris, *Willful Misconduct*, p. 215.

90 **Hides under the Tempe bridge**: "Dick Smith, Hall of Fame Diving Coach Dies at 88-January 5, 2006," www.swimmingworldmagazine.com/lane9/news/1020.asp

History 1943-1953

95 **Rev. Bernard Gordon**: "Rally Scheduled for Move to Build Pool for Mexican People," *State Press*, November 3, 1944.

96 **Backing of the entire nation**: Dennis Chavez Papers. Archive #394. Box 174, Folder 23: "Press Releases, 1942." University of New Mexico. Center for Southwest Research. Quoted in Marin, p. 4.

96 **Meet at 6 o'clock**: Ray Martinez, Interview with Jean Reynolds, November 16, 1999. Arizona History Museum.

97 **Supporters and detractors**: Martinez Interview.

97 **Check for $10,000**: Martinez Interview.

98 **Harkins addressing**: "Harkins Reports to Beach Committee, "*Tempe Daily News,* May, 15, 1946, p. 1.

98 **Vote on integration**: "Chamber of Commerce Favors 'Limited' Beach Admission of Mexican-Americans," *Tempe Daily News*, May 21, 1946, p. 1.

98 **Admission accorded to all**: "Beach Committee Acts on Policy Change Today," *Tempe Daily News*, May 22, 1946, p. 1.

99 **Dean Grimes letter**: "To Members of the Tempe Beach Board," May 24, 1946 (ME CHI RM 245) Hayden Chicano Research Collection. This collection is in the Luhrs Reading Room.

99 **Crumpler letter**: "To the Tempe Beach Committee," May 13, 1946 (CMSM 570) Hayden Chicano Collection. Also in the Luhrs Reading Room.

100 **Check for $2500**: Ray Martinez interview. Although the Mexican-American veterans won their battle to integrate the pool, the story does not end happily for some. Elizabeth Montanez Rivera, Danny Rodriguez's niece, revealed in her oral history tape that her uncle ended up moving away from Tempe. He couldn't find a job in town after winning his fight against the old guard at Tempe Beach. Interviewed by John Akers, March 18, 2003, OHT 208. Tempe History Museum.

101 **THS swim class**: Marvin Williams remembers his physed class, which included Mexican-American students, adding swimming at Tempe Beach to its activities at about this time.

101 **Manny Oliveras**: Tempe Beach Exhibition Notebook, THM.

102 **Pools in the south**: Adam Nossiter, "Unearthing a Town Pool, and Not for Whites Only," *New York Times*, September 18, 2006. http://www.nytimes.com/2006/09/18/us/18pool.html?pagewanted=print&_r=0. Thanks to my friend Zohreh Saunders for sending me this article.

102 **Seeing black people**: Phone Interview, Cindy Whatley, 2012. Thanks to Daf for putting Cindy in touch with me.

Death at Tempe Beach

103 **Mystery, horror, and fear:** Wikipedia's description.

103 **6:30 pm...**: "Tragedy Mars Beach's Long Safety Record," *Tempe Daily News*, April 26, 1945 and "Soldier Dies Trapped in Pool," *Phoenix Gazette*, April 26, 1945.

104 **Looking out the window**: Paul Aldridge, Telephone Interview with the author, 2012. All subsequent quotes from Paul are taken from this interview.

105 **Father dived into the pool**: Joe Spracale, Email, June 23, 2012.

107 **Tea baths to relieve them**: Joannie (Johnson) Hartman, "Remember Tempe, AZ When," Facebook thread.

Other Voices

Swimming for Tempe Beach

109 **The haze that he peddled through**: Herb McClure's memory was reported to me by Eldon Smith during our interview.

109 **Water freaks**: Joe P. Spracale, Interview with John H. Akers, Oral History Tape 224, August 11, 2003. Joe referred to himself as a "water freak" in this interview.

112 **He had pulleys installed**: Emil Kass, Telephone Interview, May 13, 2013.

112 **Full schedule**: "Dick Smith Gym, PCC Win Junior AAU Swim Titles," *Tempe Daily News*, July 28, 1958; "Senior AAU Warm-Up Dual Meet with Roosevelt Pool," *Tempe Daily News*, August 6, 1958; "Tempe Swimmers Score 24 ½ Points in Jr. Olympics," *Tempe Daily News,* July 21, 1958; "Tempe Winner of Three-Way Swimming Meet," *Tempe Daily News*, July 3, 1958; Eldon Smith Interview.

113 **Twenty-three swimmers**: "Swim Hosts," *Tempe Daily News*, June 17, 1958. From right, standing by the board: Cathy Mitchell, Cherrie Vincent, Pat Whalen Gary Richardson, Chuck Holly, Eldon Smith. On ladder, bottom up: Patsy Branagan, Veronica Peralta, Candy Lewis, Penny Poole, Sylvia Peralta, Jackie Richardson, Elissa Montgomery, Jackie Herren, Linda Oakley, Alan Holly, Charles Welch, Jim Ulery, Robert Horton, Teddy May, Mike Whalen, John Montgomery and Tom I'Ason.

113 **Freestyle start**: "Tempe Swimmer Places," *Tempe Daily News*, July 25, 1958.

113 **Green and gold banner**: "Spracale's Swim Stars Show Sign," *Tempe Daily News*, July 19, 1958.

113 **Candy and Eldon**: "Trophy Triumphs," *Tempe Daily News*, August 25, 1958.

116 **Highlighted swimmers**: "Smith, Holly Win Points for Tempe Swimming Team," *Tempe Daily News*, July 14, 1958.

116 **Sole girl**: "Tempe Squad to Compete in Phoenix Meet," *Tempe Daily News*, 1958.

116 **Names**: See, for example, the results of the Tempe Beach-hosted Junior AAU meet on page 4 of the July 24th, 1958, *TDN*.

116 **Team called back**: "Swimming Team to Stage Initial Drill at Tempe Beach on Monday," *Tempe Daily News*, May, 3 1962.

116 **Intra-squad**: "Intra-Squad Meet to Prepare for Arizona Relays," *Tempe Daily News*, June 5, 1962.

116 **Highly creditable**: "Sixths Recorded by City Swimmers," *Tempe Daily News*, June 11, 1962.

117 **Later meets**: "Tempe Beach Swim Team to Enter Mesa Age Group Meet," *Tempe Daily News*, June 13, 1962; "Beach Swimmers Travel to Tucson," *Tempe Daily News,* June 21, 1962; "Seven Tempeans Swim in Tucson," *Tempe Daily News*, July 13, 1962; "To the Victors, the Spoils," *Tempe Daily News*, July 9, 1962, 10; "Holly, Statz Shine for Tempe Beach in Swim Meeting," *Tempe Daily News*, July 30, 1962.

117 **End of the season picture**: "Climax Season," *Tempe Daily News*, August 23, 1962.

119 **Frogs' eggs**: Tom Ditsworth, Email, May 11, 2012.

121 **Headlines**: "Student Stabbed to Death in Dark," *Tempe Daily News*, September 22, 1966. As I looked at Laura Bernstein's picture on page 6 of the newspaper article 47 years after this event, I realized she looks nothing like me. As I was flipping to that page, I must have passed the picture of me on page 3 (I had a weekly column then) and conflated the two pictures in my mind. The memory of students at school that day saying the murderer mistook Laura for me is highly unreliable.

121 **Sister's memoir**: Jane Bernstein, *Bereft: A Sister's Story* (New York: North Point Press, 2000). This is a beautifully-written memoir. The details of the case, including these quotes from Mumbaugh and the detective, may be found on pages 182-201.

122 **Four times in the body**: Bernstein, p. 11.

124 **Daf**: Comment during interview with Chuck Holly.

124 **Entrenched in that stuff**: Joe Spracale interview, OH 224.

124 **'ceptin not green**: Tom Ditsworth, Email, February 16, 2012.

125 **Memory of Marv**: Frank Downey, Facebook message, June 10, 2012.

The Synchronized Swim Team

127 **Series of three**: Margaret (Winsor) Maciborka, Telephone Interview, April 23, 2013. All quotes from Margaret are taken from this interview.

128 **Always shiny**: Wendy Cole, conversation, March 3, 2013.

128 **17 girls**: "Swim Show Set at Tempe Beach," *Tempe Daily News*, July 24, 1962. The girls on the team were Barbara Godbey, Lynn Marie Gustafson, Nancy Leach, Mary Lehto, Sylvia Lehto, Laura Sellards, Starr Sellards, Mary Jane Wegner, Margaret

Winsor, Linda Carnal, Louise Vogel, Connie Carlson, Judy Davis, Sue Foster, Jean Foster, Colleen Kigin and Jeanne Welman.

128 **Two months after**: Millie Loughrige, Interview.

128 **Conditioning**: Millie Loughrige.

129 **The more difficult moves**: Valerie McMillion, Telephone Interview, 2012. All subsequent quotes from Valerie are taken from this interview.

129 **Star, natural in the water**: Linda (Carnal) Whatley

129 **Winning everything**: Mary Jane (Wegner) Torok

130 **Watch the leader**: Valerie McMillion

131 **Red and white suits**: "Beach Swimmers Give Show Again Tonight," *Tempe Daily News,* July 26, 1962. Descriptions of the show come from this article and from "Swim Show Set at Tempe Beach."

132 **Junior stunt meet**: "Beach Swimmers in Synchronized Meet on July 31," *Tempe Daily News*, July 30, 1962.

132 **275 people; Elissa; Nincompoops**: "Beach Swimmers Give Show Again Tonight."

133 **Huge fun, Stair-step**: Margaret (Winsor) Maciborka.

Guarding at Tempe Beach

139 **Champagne water**: Joe Spracale, Interview, OH 224.

140 **Fig-eater beetles**: Carl "Bug Man" Olson, email, March, 2013. People called these Japanese beetles, but Carl Olson, an entomologist at U of A, assured me they were fig-eaters, often called June bugs.

141 **Water pressure**: "Large Drop in Pressure Last Night," *Tempe Daily News*, July 16, 1963.

142 **Red Cross sponsored**: Sarah Martin, 11.

144 **You can do it**: JoAnn (Voss) Brown, "Remember Tempe, AZ When," Facebook thread, 2012.

144 **Silver dollar**: Janice (Hollis) Strickland, "Remember Tempe, AZ When," Facebook thread, 2012.

150 **Bench**: Joe Spracale, Interview, OHT 224.

Fourth-Day Water
Memoir

155 **AAU champion**: "Diving Team Sets Saturday Tryouts," *Tempe Daily News,* May 31, 1963, p. 1. In memory of last year's "coup," Daf and I are referred to as the team's "leading lights."

156 **Statistics**: "1,000 Take Part in Beach Instruction," *Tempe Daily News*, June 21, 1962, p. 1.

158 **3 meter title**: "Sally Cole Takes State 3 Meter Springboard Title," *Tempe Daily News*, July 29, 1963, p. 4.

160 **Shooting of lifeguard**: "Beach Lifeguard Suffers Gunshot Wound In Arm," *Tempe Daily News,* June 26, 1963, p. 1.

161 **Cut-offs**: "Cut-offs Banned at Tempe Beach," *Tempe Daily News*, July 17, 1963.

161 **New pool**: "Beach Opening Begins at Dedication Tonight," *Tempe Daily News*, May 29, 1964, p. 1.

History

163 **5 or 6 families**: Daf, during interview with Alex Arredondo.

164 **50 yards**: Marvin Williams, Interview.

164 **Boxing**: Email from Bill Lee, May 24, 2013.

164 **Typical commencement night**: Michael Wilson Kelly, "Tempe Beach Park Swimming Pool Facility: A Documentation for Posterity," January 1999, p. 4. This document is in the THM.

165 **Class of 1961 Quiz**: A copy of this quiz was given to me by Chuck Holly during his interview. Answers: 1. Phil 2. Alligators 3. 600,000 4. 1 5. 1964 6. Chuck Holly 7. Divvied them up; went to Monti's 8. Head of Parks and Recreation 9. Yes or no 10. Yes or no 11. Joe, Marvin, Chuck, Don, Paul, Eldon, John, Alex, Dan, Allen…. 12. Women's

165 **Marriage proposals**: Harry Mitchell, "Document for Posterity," p. 4.

166 **Met wives**: Emails from Chuck and Tom.

166 **Ritual events**: Harry Mitchell, "Document," p. 4.

166 **Memory of Harold**: Mark Bryson, Facebook message, July 1, 2012.

Other Voices

Bullets Over Tempe Beach

171 **Allen's first-hand account**: Allen Adams, Phone Interview, April 15, 2013.

Alligators in the Baby Pool

173 **2010 alligator story**: Mary Ellen Resendez, "Alligator Brought in to Help Clean Up Tempe Town Lake," July 23, 2010: http://www.abc15.com/dpp/news/region_southeast_valley/tempe/ alligator-brought-in-to-eat-tempe-town-lakes-dying-fish

174 **Alligator roundups**: Photograph Caption, *Tempe Daily News*, June 28, 1963.

175 **Part of a haul**: "4 'Gators Are Found at Pool," *Tempe Daily News*, June 28, 1963.

175 **Story of alligator farm**: David Lomeli, Interview with Steve Cole, February 25, 2011. All subsequent quotes from David come from this interview.

175 **Closing of the farm**: David McDowell, Email, March, 2012.

177 **That very night**: *Tempe Daily News,* "Four 'Gators."

Fifth-Day Water
Memoir

186 **Back flip**: "Recent TUHS Graduate Dies in Lake Accident," *Tempe Daily News*, June 20, 1966. James Watson died after doing a "40-foot back flip into Canyon Lake."

Swept Away

189 **Turnout**: "Biggest Turnout in Tempe History," *Tempe Daily News*, October 30, 1963.

189 **Wasn't framed that way**: "State Bond Meets," *Tempe Daily News*, October 12, 1963, p. 1; "Turnout Poor Thursday for 2 Bond Meets," *Tempe Daily News*, October 18, 1963, p. 1; "Water, Sewer, Parks Await Bond Issues for 9 Million," *Tempe Daily News*, October 28, 1963.

190 **Minutes**: Minutes of Special Council Meeting, Parks and Recreation Board, June 20, 1963. Minutes of both the City Council and Special Parks and Recreation Board may be found at the City Clerk's office.

190 **Signs of wear**: Parks and Recreation Monthly Report, August, 1963.

190 **Water issues**: Parks and Recreation Monthly Report, August, 1963.

190 **Blueprints**: Special Parks and Recreation Board and Council Committee Meeting, November 23, 1963.

191 **Plan A**: Parks and Recreation Board and Council Meeting, December 3, 1963.

191 **Plan B sketch and article**: "Beach Plans Listed," *Tempe Daily News*, February 7, 1964, p. 1.

192 **New competitive length**: Harry Mitchell, Phone Interview, March, 2013.

192 **Benefits**: Michael Wilson Kelly, "Tempe Beach Park Swimming Pool Facility: A Documentation for Posterity," January, 1999, p. 2.

193 **Drowning**: "Boy Drowns Sunday in Tempe Beach Pool; Revival Efforts Fail," *Tempe Daily News*, May 31, 1966, p. 1. This occurred almost two years to the day from the pool's opening.

193 **Dire need of updates**: Ron Pies, Retired Director of Parks and Recreation Department, "Document," p. 5.

193 **Lack of use**: Skip Bryant, "Document," p. 5.

193 **Regional draw**: "Document," p. 3.

193 **Little city pool**: Rudy Campbell, Telephone Interview, March, 2013.

193 **Collective highlights of old pool**: "Document," p. 3.

194 **Historic value of the place**: Pies, "Document," p. 5.

194 **Sorely missed**: "Document," p. 3.

PHOTO CREDITS

P. 9 Courtesy of Tempe History Museum (Harold Vogel Collection)

P. 12 Courtesy of Tempe History Museum

P. 17 Courtesy of Steve Ramos

P. 25 Courtesy of Beatriz Vianna

P. 51 Courtesy of Tempe History Museum

P. 53 Courtesy of Tempe History Museum

P. 66 Photo taken at kiosk at 13th and Ash, Tempe

P. 67 Courtesy of Joe Spracale

P. 107 Courtesy of Tempe History Museum

P. 114 Photos courtesy of Joe Spracale. Photos taken by Larry McGrath and Bob Connolly.

P. 115 Photos courtesy of Joe Spracale. Photos taken by Larry McGrath and Bob Connolly.

P. 118 Charles Hilgeman photo

P. 127 Charles Hilgeman photo

P. 137 Courtesy of Chuck Holly

P. 142 Courtesy of Joe Spracale

P. 144 Courtesy of Alex Arredondo

P. 145 Courtesy of Joe Spracale

P. 147 Courtesy of John Hollis

P. 148 Tempe Daily News photo courtesy of Tom Voss

P. 163 Courtesy of Joe Spracale

P. 166 Photo by Tom Cole

P. 173 Drawing by Stephen Cole

P. 187 Photo by Tom Cole

P. 189 Courtesy of Tempe History Museum

23938358R00121

Made in the USA
Lexington, KY
28 June 2013